In Celebration of Our Survival

For years, aboriginal people have been studied, observed, and written about, usually by members of the non-native community. The present volume has been written, compiled, and edited by aboriginal peoples from British Columbia who, in telling their own stories, celebrate the survival of the distinct cultures of the First Nations people in the face of decades of colonization and attempts at assimilation.

The editors of this volume called upon native individuals from all walks of life who were recognized by their own people for their knowledge and experience. The contributors were simply asked to tell their story and to write about what they felt was important in creating a portrait of their people. The result is a rich and multifaceted collection of writings, poetry, and art touching on a wide range of topics, including the constitution, education, language, culture, and native activism. It is a timely book which while celebrating the survival of native culture also informs us about the issues confronting native peoples, about the challenges they face in regaining control of their destiny, and about their struggle to maintain their culture.

Edited by Doreen Jensen and Cheryl Brooks

In Celebration of Our Survival
The First Nations of British Columbia

UBCPress
Vancouver

ISBN 0-7748-0402-5 (hardcover)
ISBN 0-7748-0403-3 (paperback)

Canadian Cataloguing in Publication Data

Main entry under title:
In celebration of our survival

Also issued as BC studies, no. 89, 1991
Includes bibliographical references.
ISBN 0-7748-0402-5 (bound).
ISBN 0-7748-0403-3 (pbk.)

1. Indians of North America – British Columbia.
2. Canadian literature (English) – Indian authors.*
I. Jensen, Doreen, 1933-. II. Brooks, Cheryl.
III. Title: BC studies.
E78.B9152 1991   971.1'00497   C91-091525-3

Royalties from this book will be donated to the First Nations
House of Learning to help fund future publications.

UBC Press
University of British Columbia
6344 Memorial Rd
Vancouver, BC V6T 1Z2
(604) 822-3259
Fax (604) 822-6083

Contents

Foreword   3

Preface   8

Articles

Artist's Statement and Profile   WALTER HARRIS   15

In Time Immemorial   DAISY SEWID-SMITH   16

Conspiracy of Legislation: The Suppression of
Indian Rights in Canada
                    CHIEF JOE MATHIAS and GARY R. YABSLEY   34

Policy Development for Museums: A First Nations Perspective
                                              E. RICHARD ATLEO   48

Assimilation Tools: Then and Now   SHIRLEY JOSEPH   65

Sechelt Women and Self-Government   THERESA M. JEFFRIES   81

I Invite Honest Criticism: An Introduction   RON HAMILTON   89

A Biography of Sorts   RON HAMILTON   100

A Study of Education in Context   E. RICHARD ATLEO   104

Understanding Native Activism   STEVEN POINT   124

Artist's Statement   DAVID NEEL   131

Life on the 18th Hole   DAVID NEEL   132

The Value of First Nations Languages   PATRICK KELLY   141

The Children of Tomorrow's Great Potlatch   ERNIE CREY   150

Native Spirituality, Past, Present and Future

                                LEONARD GEORGE   160

Poems BY RON HAMILTON

Our Voice — Our Struggle (7), Preparing to Fly (13), From A Bridge (33), Paper Garrotes (46), Box Of Darkness (62), A Part Apart (80), Our Story Not History (87), A Collection of Poems (93-99), Fourth World (120), Michelle (121), Today In Class (Every Day) (130), Three Musts (140), My Blanket, My Story (149), More Than Us (159), Telling (169)

Art

Walter Harris 'Celebration of Life' (14), Ron Hamilton 'Life And Death And Life' (88) and 'Ii-ishsuu-ilth' design (92), David Neel 'Life on the 18th Hole' (following page 130)

The generous assistance of the Leon and Thea Koerner Foundation, the Museum of Anthropology, University of British Columbia, and the Hamber Foundation, in the publication of this special issue is gratefully acknowledged.

In Celebration of Our Survival

Foreword

This journal has given attention to the First Nations of British Columbia virtually since its founding in 1969. Special issues focusing on First Nations affairs have twice been published ("Indians in British Columbia," No. 19, Autumn 1973; "British Columbia: A Place for Aboriginal Peoples?" No. 57, Spring 1983) and individual articles concerned with native Indian culture, history, and experience have appeared regularly in its pages.

Consistently informative, carefully researched, and widely read, this material shared one other obvious characteristic: it was in its entirety produced by non-aboriginal scholars, investigators, and commentators. By early 1990 this seemed a situation palpably in need of change. First Nations people in British Columbia and around the globe were increasingly asserting their right to speak for themselves. In many cases they had been telling their stories for years. The community at large was displaying an unprecedented willingness to listen to what they had to say. That they should have space to speak for themselves in this publication — especially given the fact that its contributors had for so long been writing about and even for them — seemed an altogether timely and reasonable proposition.

Adoption of this view, it must immediately be added, in no sense meant capitulation to the idea that only members of a group, society, or culture have authority to comment on the affairs of that group, society, or culture. *BC Studies* remains convinced that investigators of competence and sensitivity can contribute constructively to discussion of a society or culture whether they are affiliated with it or not. But the journal also thinks that even observers of that exemplary sort are not automatically entitled to monopolize what gets said. Societies and cultures should, where possible, be able to speak for themselves. Only then can their vision of their experience be presented in the (relatively) unmediated way justice and accuracy demand. Only then can those "outside" these societies get the sort of direct testimony concerning that vision which is essential to the building of a well-rounded and comprehensive understanding of it and of the social whole to which it is linked. And — perhaps most important of all — only then can

3

the world beyond those societies see something of the toughness and co-hesion which has undergirded and made possible their survival. Shot through with commitment and authenticity, the writing, poetry, and art brought together here do not, then, merely inform: they offer extraordinarily eloquent testimony to the dignity, sense of self, and simple strength which has allowed the culture of their creators to persist and endure under circumstances which it would be a gratuitously offensive understatement to describe as difficult. It is an honour to be able to present them to our readers.

* * *

Anxious to ensure that the form and content of this issue would be reflective of First Nations sensibilities in as many respects as possible, *BC Studies* invited the distinguished Gitksan artist, historian, author, and activist Doreen Jensen to act as its guest editor. Mrs. Jensen in turn arranged to collaborate with Sto:lo organizer and writer Cheryl Brooks. Experienced, articulate, and strongly committed to the culture and traditions of their people, they have brought together precisely the sort of balanced, coherent, stimulating, and varied set of papers, artwork, and poetry necessary to fulfillment of the volume's purpose.

* * *

Born and raised in the Cariboo by her mother Agnes, who came from the Lorenzetto family of the Sto:lo Nation, and by her stepfather Arthur, who was of Lillooet ancestry, Cheryl Brooks attended high school and then worked her way up to the position of executive director of the Quesnel Tillicum Society's Native Friendship Centre, where she oversaw the development and delivery of a number of social and economic programs for aboriginal people and communities. During her time there she served on the Board of Directors of the provincial and national associations and was elected as the first woman president of the National Association of Friendship Centres. Mrs. Brooks has also been a member of a number of other social justice organizations including Human Rights and Civil Liberties and Native Women's groups and was the first Canadian native woman to be selected as a member of the Duke of Edinburgh's study conference which studied government, business, and labour relations in Australia.

She then relocated to the Lower Mainland and worked for the federal Department of the Secretary of State where she was responsible for policy development and the delivery of programs to support native political organizations, social and cultural development projects, and native communications activities. She is now working in the federal Department of Western Economic Diversification, where she assists companies with their business development.

When Mrs. Brooks was given her Sto:lo name, Patholwet, the elders who served as witnesses at the ceremony instructed her to use her gifts of communication to weave bonds between people, just as the ancestor whose name she was receiving had been a weaver of blankets and baskets.

In 1981 Mrs. Brooks met Doreen Jensen. Since then they have collaborated on a number of projects related to native art and culture and have co-authored several articles and proposals.

In addition to her full-time job and family responsibilities, Mrs. Brooks volunteers with community organizations and works as a freelance writer and consultant. Mrs. Brooks and her husband Conan live in Coquitlam with their four children.

*   *   *

Hahl Yee is the name that was given to Doreen Jensen by her family. The name belongs to the Killer Whale family crest from the House of Geel, of the Fireweed Clan, her mother's lineage.

Mrs. Jensen's early training began in the oral history tradition, learning the language (Gitksan), songs, legends, and customs from her parents and grandparents. Her formal schooling began in a two-room day school in Kispiox. At the age of ten she left her family to attend Alberni Residential School for two years, returning to a newly integrated public high school in Prince Rupert. After leaving high school she returned to her home territory to work.

Mrs. Jensen realized early in life that native people were not being heard; that their voice was silenced when discussing their destiny. In 1963, she began what would become a personal and professional journey to help change that. Conversant in her culture, and drawn to artistic expression, she chose to use the creative arts as a vehicle for conveying traditional cultural messages. In her view, it is through art that culture is made tangible, and it is through art that native people can communicate across cultures.

Mrs. Jensen is an artist, teacher, historian, community organizer and political activist. She is a founding member of many organizations, including 'Ksan Association and the Society of Canadian Artists of Native Ancestry, and she was instrumental in organizing the Third National Native Indian Artists Symposium in Hazelton in 1983. Her work concentrates on bringing native voices to the forefront and finding ways to facilitate individual and cultural expression. She conceived of the Robes of Power exhibit, book, and video, wherein many artists and elders were able to share their cultural experience as expressed through the creation and use of the ceremonial robes. As a book-builder, she researched materials for publication of books for the Kitanmax School of Northwest Coast Indian Art, which again gave expression to native voices.

Because of her community involvement, her time to create her own art is limited, but still her work has been exhibited and collected by public institutions. Her work is appreciated for its beauty and strength, and for its ability to combine individual expression with cultural meaning and purpose. She continues to be involved in community service as chairperson with the Gitksan and Wet'suwet'en Vancouver Support Group, as a member of the Vancouver Sub-Committee on Cultural Diversity, and as a member of the Board of Trustees of the National Museum of Nature in Ottawa.

Her work has won her the Professional Native Women's Association's highest award, that of the Golden Eagle Feather, in recognition of her outstanding contribution to her community.

In 1987, she was given a special honour. At his last potlatch in Campbell River, B.C., the late Chief James Auld Sewid and his family bestowed upon her a name which had belonged to an aunt of Chief Sewid. The name given was Eik'awiga, which means Precious Jewel.

Mrs. Jensen and her husband Vergil make their home in South Surrey. They have four children and four grandchildren.

Allan Smith
Editor, *BC Studies*

Our Voice — Our Struggle

We are struggling to find our voice,
The right tone, the right pitch,
The right speed, the right code
The right thoughts, the right words

We are struggling to find the voice,
To say how long we've waited to speak,
To say we're tired of waiting so long,
To say we're tired — and frustrated

Struggling, we wax nostalgic,
Struggling for a new reading of history,
Struggling for human status,
Struggling just to be heard.

We are struggling against false accusations

Fall 1984,
at Balaatsad

Preface

It was in the spring, approximately a year ago, that we began work on this project. The year 1990 was being heralded as the dawning of a new decade of communication. The Berlin wall was coming down, and the East and West German people were celebrating joyously. In South Africa Nelson Mandela was being released from prison and the hopes for peace in that land were soaring. Mikhail Gorbachev was recognized for his efforts to end the Cold War. It seemed there was much to celebrate in the world, and as we watched the German people tearing down the Berlin wall and gathering in the streets, we wondered what the aboriginal people had to be glad about. As we thought of our history and what is happening today, it came to us that even after decades of colonization and attempts at assimilation, First Nations People have survived as distinct and dynamic cultures with great prospects for the future. Our very survival is cause for celebration. So we started with the title, "In Celebration of Our Survival." Then, as is customary in the feast halls and gatherings of our people, we called upon the learned speakers, the orators from many locations and walks of life to document the business of this celebration with their words. It had to be a special invitation as we were not only asking them to witness this occasion; we were challenging them to do it in a new way. Many of these people are known for their ability to stand in a gathering and extemporaneously speak for hours with clarity, logic and emotion, but to write it down would be a new experience. We assured contributors that we were not so much looking for the ability to flawlessly apply the non-traditional tool of writing as we were seeking the knowledge and wisdom of the true experts on aboriginal issues.

Aboriginal people have been the subject of much study and comment by the academic community for many years. Indeed, *BC Studies* itself has published two previous editions — Autumn 1973 (no. 19) and Spring 1983 (no. 57) — devoted to the topic. This special issue is, however, distinguished from its predecessors because all of the contributions have been written and the compilation and editing have been done by aboriginal peoples from British Columbia. It is further distinguished by the fact that the contributors are not all academics; most are native individuals who are recognized by their own people for their knowledge and experience. The other major difference is in the form of presentation: the authors have not striven to present only objective and factual information but have described the human emotions and reactions to the events and situations described. While readers will learn a lot of new facts, they will also, it is hoped, acquire a greater insight into intangibles such as the spirits, hopes, and dreams that are an integral part of aboriginal life and aboriginal issues in British Columbia.

In the invitation to contributors we said:

For years and years we as aboriginal people have been studied, observed and written about, generally by non-aboriginal writers. We have been portrayed in a variety of ways, from being ignorant savages to victims of the dominant societies and sometimes even as fascinating anthropological specimens. While all of us who have been in the feast halls and have been involved in Indian organizations have heard the correct versions of our history and our leaders' plans and visions for the future, many people have not had the opportunity to be there and to hear this information first hand, without the biases and slants of observers and interpreters. . . . This letter is to invite you, as an aboriginal person from British Columbia with a lot of knowledge, experience and credibility, to help create a self-portrait of our peoples. A portrait that will tell people who we really are, what we are doing, and our plans, hopes and dreams. We want to portray our strengths, accomplishments, contributions and visions. We need to educate people about the multiplicity of issues we are addressing, the challenge to regain control of our destinies, and the struggle to maintain our culture and perhaps even to tell others how they can support us in our efforts.

As the months passed, events transpired which made it even more clearly imperative that we as aboriginal people communicate and create dialogue with the dominant society through whatever vehicles are available. The failure of the Meech Lake constitutional accord to bring Quebec into the Canadian constitution was largely attributed to the refusal of Elijah Harper, a native member of Manitoba's legislative assembly, to support the accord until commitments were made by the government to Canada's aboriginal people. This created much animosity against natives. By the summer of 1990 the Mohawk people of Kanesatake and Kanawake, seeking government commitment to resolution of aboriginal issues and the prevention of the construction of a golf course on traditional lands, became embroiled in an armed standoff with the Quebec and Canadian governments. Supportive road blocks and information blockades were put in place by other natives, particularly in British Columbia. The standoff lasted three months and left a bitter aftertaste of covert hostilities, resentment, anger, and misunderstanding among natives and non-natives alike.

As we planned for this publication, we debated how we should limit and focus the content, but ultimately decided that perhaps that has been part of the problem in the past: native people have always been asked for their comments on and contributions to established agenda topics rather than simply being requested to tell their own story. So our contributors were invited to write about what they personally felt was important in painting a portrait of our people. What we learned as the articles were submitted and as we talked with many people who were not able to contribute because of other commitments is that it is not possible to paint a fully detailed portrait in a single volume. We hope, however, that we have at least provided a window through which viewers will see enough points of interest that they will be motivated to go outside into direct contact with B.C.'s aboriginal peoples and to learn for themselves what is not included in this portrait.

Walter Harris, well-known Gitksan artist, contributes a three-tone print representing the centrality of life and importance of family. The print, a product of the period when the artist was awaiting open-heart surgery, depicts a whale giving birth while watched by her mate.

Daisy Sewid-Smith relates the events of her people's earliest contacts with the Europeans. While conveying the first hand observations of her ancestors she also quotes from the records of the visitors. Her article is a poignant reminder of the long history of suffering by her people which also conveys the strength and resiliency of the people.

Joe Mathias and Gary Yabsley review the legislation that has enabled government to suppress Indian rights in Canada. They strongly refute the popular misconception that Indian people gave up their rights in order to enjoy the benefits of the white man's lifestyle, and provide clear evidence of the endurance of the aboriginal people.

Richard Atleo summarizes a study of aboriginal educational achievements and the external and internal factors which effected those achievements. He suggests that improvements in educational achievement by native people coincided with a major attitudinal shift in society whereby the dominant society stopped excluding natives from the general milieu. In his examination of factors positively affecting Indian education he provides a fresh perspective on this much studied topic.

Shirley Joseph evaluates the government's efforts to assimilate aboriginal people through legislation dealing with government regulations regarding the definitions of who is Indian. She outlines the continuing problems that result from flawed and intrusive legislation that tries to tell aboriginal people who is permitted to be included in their family backgrounds.

Theresa Jeffries provides an overview of the Sechelt band self-government arrangement. She focuses on the traditional and contemporary roles and contributions of Sechelt women to self-government and expresses much optimism for the future.

Ron Hamilton has been writing poetry in private for many years about people and events in the aboriginal community. His article talks about his writing, while the poems themselves appear throughout the collection.

Richard Atleo, in a second contribution, maintains that museums that house aboriginal collections need to incorporate First Nations viewpoints in their policy development. Richard submits that repatriation is the issue which will create the greatest controversy in museum policy, and he suggests some guidelines to be considered in developing such policy.

Steven Point and David Neel examine the rise of militancy and the expressions of rage and frustration by native people engaged in the struggle for change. They summarize the milestones that have led to this situation and stress the urgent need for serious dialogue and commitment to resolving the many outstanding grievances of aboriginal people. David has also contributed a print he created to serve as a reminder of the struggle of all First Nations people.

Patrick Kelly's article on First Nations languages stresses the importance of language as a vehicle for creating understanding in a world where change is the norm. He describes the challenges of ensuring language survival and articulates the importance of the survival of the many aboriginal languages for native and non-native people alike.

Ernie Crey also discusses education, but in the context of the impact of residential schools and in terms of the way removal of native children from their communities created apprehension. He describes the devastating consequences of these actions and then tells how and what improvements are being made by B.C.'s native people.

Leonard George provides some insight into the contrasts between the value systems of natives and non-natives. By sharing information about native spirituality and traditional practices he puts forward some easily understood ideas for improving the lives of both individuals and societies.

Now, as we have been taught in our feast halls and gatherings, we must recognize and thank all those who have assisted us and contributed to the celebration of our survival. We first thank the Creator for the gift of life, then thank our ancestors for the strength and vision they passed to us. We thank the contributors who have given their writings to this publication.

We thank our leaders past and present for their tenacity and work on our people's behalf. We thank those of you who wanted to contribute but could not because of other pressing commitments. We also offer special thanks and recognition to the many non-native people who have assisted and continue to assist us in our struggle for survival: Drs. Allan Smith and Michael Ames of *BC Studies*, who offered us the opportunity to guest edit this special edition; Henny Winterton of *BC Studies*, who provided administrative support; and Thomas Berger, Paul Tennant, Stephen Hume, Douglas Cole and Ira Chaikin, who, among many others, have advanced the understanding of our people through their writing. We also thank you, the readers, for participating in our first written celebration. Finally and most importantly we thank our families for their patience, love, and support as we took time away from them to work on this project.

It is true, as you will have learned, that our people have suffered tremendous assaults on their very being, but, as the late George Manuel, author of the *Fourth World*, (1974) said, "It is time that we as Indian people declare victory, that we have survived."[1]

We welcome you to our Celebration.

Doreen Jensen and Cheryl Brooks

[1] Quoted from a speech by Mr. Manuel, in the film "The Land is Our Culture," produced by the Union of B.C. Indian Chiefs, 1975.

Preparing To Fly

I was thrilled speechless,
Excited beyond words.
Tongue thick, numb, dumb
Rushing thoughts to no-one in particular.

The wall was coming apart!
Men strained muscles.
Children pecked with fingernails,
Pencils, screwdrivers, hammers and spikes.

Women wailed and railed,
And beat bare fists
Until raw.
The wall was penetrated!

Here and there holes appeared,
Just pin holes at first.
The windows and doorways
Let light through one side to another.

People perched along the top,
Preparing to fly,
Scratching with their clawed feet.
Dust, pebbles, boulders, slabs.

The wall, a trembling victim,
Crumbled in living rooms around
The world.
A victory for the whole world.

We all rejoiced without restraint.
Restraint had no role here.
We celebrated openly.
Some few perhaps celebrated privately.

The wall was standing still,
But around the world its demise
Was cause for celebration, tears, joy!
It swayed, buckled, prepared to fall.

Distant friends, strangers to prison,
Thought holes through the wall.
Friends loved cracks in cement,
They wished the foundation to pieces.

One full year later, I still tremble.

Winter 1990,
at Musqueam

Celebration of Life

by Walter Harris

Artist's Statement and Profile

WALTER HARRIS

WALTER HARRIS was born and raised in Kispiox village and is a member of the Gitksan nation in northern British Columbia. Walter has been successful in almost every venture he has undertaken. Before his career as an artist, Walter's energy, talents, and determination contributed to his success in various industries. In 1957 Walter was given his maternal uncle's hereditary name of "Geel." Receiving this name and its responsibilities established him as the recognized leader of Kispiox among the chiefs of the Gitksan nation.

While taking part in the construction of a replica of the Gitksan village now known as 'Ksan, Walter was intrigued by the forms and symbolisms of Northwest Coast Indian art. This awakened interest led him to want to learn more, so he enrolled in the newly formed 'Kitanmax School of Northwest Coast Indian Art in 1969. He studied and mastered jewellery under Jack Leyland, and wood carving under Duane Pasco and Doug Cranmer, and attended seminars on Northwest Coast graphic design given by Bill Holm. Walter eventually developed his talents to a point of being named senior instructor of wood sculpture at 'Ksan — a post which he proudly held for many years.

As Walter mastered his art, he created his own unique style which adheres closely to the Gitksan traditions. The public recognition and appreciation of his artistic talents and versatility have allowed him to continue pursuing his career in art. Throughout the years numerous select pieces of Mr. Harris have found their way into the public and private collections of well-known authorities and collectors in Northwest Coast Indian Art from many countries around the world. A highlight of his art career came in 1978 when he was appointed to the Fine Arts Committee of Canada, which selects significant artifacts to be purchased by the federal government.

In 1987, Walter's artistic endeavours and productivity came to an abrupt end as a result of a stroke. Through the encouragement and support of his family and his own persistence he was able slowly to begin a long journey toward recovery, only to receive a further setback in the form of major heart surgery in 1990. Today Walter, fully recovered, is in good health, and his artistic production has been re-established to its full form.

Walter's recent serigraph entitled "Celebration of Life," made during his trying times, captures his view of what life should be.

In Time Immemorial

DAISY SEWID-SMITH

"Our history stretches far back into the silent past. When the great Creator came on earth and walked and talked with our people."

DAISY SEWID-SMITH was born in Alert Bay, B.C. on 28 November 1938. She is one of nine surviving children of the late Chief James Sewid. She was raised at Village Island until the age of six. Then Chief James Sewid moved to Alert Bay seeking better education for his children. Daisy attended the Alert Bay Indian Day School and then attended the first provincial integrated school in the area. When Daisy graduated she attended a Vancouver College secretarial course. On its completion she worked for the Indian Affairs Branch in Alert Bay for a number of years. Daisy was married to Lorne Smith of Turnour Island. She has two children, Gloria and Todd, and two grandchildren, Shonna and Jamie.

Daisy has written several articles for magazines, and in 1979 wrote the book "Prosecution or Persecution" for the Cape Mudge Museum. This book deals with the potlatch and the confiscation and return of the artifacts to the Kʷagut people by The Department of Indian Affairs. Daisy is presently working on her grandmother's life story with Martine Reid and developing the Liqʷala/Kʷakʷala grammar books for School District #72 in Campbell River. She has been employed by School District #72 for eleven years.

Over the years Daisy has lectured at many schools, colleges, and universities, both in the United States and Canada. She hopes to write more books in the future.

* * *

We have been fighting for our land since the time of contact. Native Indian nations all.over Canada have protested against the systematic methods used to take away our land, natural resources and even our freedom to move about in our country. The wishes and even the existence of the native nations have been totally ignored. Promises are made and constantly broken. Our history after contact is full of abuses and sorrows. It is no wonder that the history books are silent about our past. If by accident we are mentioned, it is to say we are a primitive people, with no past, no contribution, no land and above all no rights in our own country. Until quite recently, every history book written stated that North American history began with the discovery of America by Christopher Columbus and British Columbian history began with Sir Francis Drake in 1577 and Captain James Cook in 1778.

16

Many of my relatives came in contact with Captain George Vancouver in 1792 at what is now known as the Nimpkish River. At the time of contact our population was large in number. The tribes were scattered around Vancouver Island, the inland waters, and the mainland. Prior to this meeting we already had a long history in what is now known as British Columbia.

In Time Immemorial

Our history stretches far back into the silent past. When the great Creator came on earth and walked and talked with our people.

One day the great Creator told those he favoured that a great deluge was coming upon the earth. He instructed each family on how to prepare for the coming flood waters. To one family the instructions were to cover each canoe with cedar bark and cover every hole with pitch. To another family the instructions were to remain in the house and also to cover every hole with pitch. To my ancestor c̓eqəmē his instructions were to hollow out a great cedar tree and he too was to cover every hole with pitch. After he had carried out these instructions he was then to bring his wife, his daughter, and his four sons into the hollowed out cedar tree for safety. The great deluge came just as the great Creator predicted, and all but those whom he favoured perished.

After the Flood

When the flood waters subsided, the survivors left their place of safety. This place became known as the "place of descent." Every place of descent became sacred ground to the people that are now known as the Kʷaguł Nation. The place of descent of my ancestor c̓eqəmē is a place called Mit̓ap near Gilford Island. It is located at the bottom of Mount Reid. This was the place of descent of the ancestors of my people, the Qʷiqʷasut̓inux̌ʷ tribe.

When the survivors left their place of descent, they immediately started seeking other survivors. When families found one another, marriages were arranged between sons and daughters. To this day the dramatization of these first marriages plays an important part in our own tribal marriage ceremonies. After these unions the families went back to their place of descent and built a house. Soon after this a supernatural bird appeared to them. The supernatural bird was either a qulus, d̓una, or a Thunderbird. This supernatural bird stepped out of his bird form and came and lived with my people. My ancestor's daughter married ʔud̓ista, the qulus.

During the ceremony, when it was time for the groom to claim his wife, the qulus used an enormous spoon to bring his wife to his side. He held on to the handle while the bride sat inside the spoon. This became an important part of a Qʷiqʷasutinux̌ʷ marriage ceremony. To this day a dividing line can be seen on Mount Reid. This dividing line was made when the great qulus slid down the mountain to make contact with čeqəmē and his family. Our people call this dividing line k̓əxədəxʷ meaning "having parted hair."

Authority was vested in the father, the elder and patriarch of the family. He became known as the ʔuǧʷəmē or λax̌ʷəmē, meaning he was the head of the family. "The responsibility of the position was to see that the family had enough to eat and that they did not want for anything." Later this responsibility was to include protection against an enemy attack. To fulfil this task, the sons and sons-in-law hunted, fished, and worked for the Patriarch. The provisions were stored in storage boxes in the house in preparation for the winter months. Later when the population increased the whole clan worked for their ʔuǧʷəmē or λax̌ʷəmē,[1] which now meant "head chief."

As the population increased the Patriarch gave land to all his sons, except for the eldest. These sons became the ʔuǧʷəmē or λax̌ʷəmē of their own families and eventually evolved into a clan of their own.[2] The eldest son remained with the Patriarch because he was to inherit his position, land, and privileges.[3] The eldest was also to be the head ʔuǧʷəmē or λax̌ʷəmē of what was now a tribe with a large population. In later years the name of the position was changed to Giǧamē, meaning "greater than," and it was later translated by the Europeans to mean "Chief" because they saw a similarity between our society and that of the Scottish Highlanders.[4]

[1] "This was also asked by you about the early Indians. Indeed, they work for the head Chiefs of the Numaym ." Franz Boas, "Ethnology of the Kwakiutl," Based on Data Collected by George Hunt, in *Thirty-Fifth Annual Report*, Bureau of American Ethnology, 1913-1914, (Washington: Government Printing Office, 1921), 133.
"of all the different kinds of food, a little is given to the Chief by those who belong to his numaym ." *Ibid.*, 137.

[2] "And then Lalaxsendayo said that Nenologeme and his children should now form another tribe. And the name of that tribe was Elgunwe beginning that day." Ibid., 96.

[3] "for it was instituted in olden times that the head Chiefs had to keep their names, and that they could give them to no other than the eldest among their children. *Ibid.*, 83.

[4] "The social structure of the Indians was highly interesting, that of the Kwakiutl being in some respects more complex than that of the Salish. There was a definite hierarchy of society, similar in some ways to that prevailing some centuries ago in the Scottish highlands." Derek Pethick, *The Fort* (Vancouver: Mitchell Press, 1968), 6.

In some tribes the names given the clans were the names of the sons of
the first Patriarch. The original clans of the Qʷiqʷasut̓inux̌ʷ tribe were
the names of čeqamēs sons. These clans shared the same privileges because
their origin was the same. This is also true about the Wiweqē and
Wiweq̓əm clans of the Liǧʷiɬdax̌ʷ tribe. The names of these two clans
were the names of the two sons of the Liǧʷiɬdax̌ʷ Patriarch, Weqē .
These true clans would be referred to as "nəmima", meaning "coming
from the same origin."

A few of the early Patriarchs formed only one clan after the flood. These
clans formed a confederation of clans. They lived in the same territory,
but they lived in separate villages. These clans usually took the name of
their Patriarch or a name that described who they were. They did not own
the same land and resources.[5] The land and resources of these clans were
the territory around their "place of descent" after the flood. These clans
did not have the same privileges because they did not have the same place
of descent. They were not nəməyəm or kinsmen.

Before European Contact

As the population increased in British Columbia, tribal wars broke out.
It was during this period that the clans decided to form a more powerful
front by forming an alliance with other clans. True clans moved back into
the head clan's village. Large tribes were formed consisting of (1) clans,
(2) clans and alliances, and (3) a confederation of clans. Clan ownership
of land, resources, and privileges remained the same. Not all clans joined
other clans at this time. A few still lived in separate villages but were living
close together for protection and for potlatching.[6]

The tribes and clans of the Indian nations of British Columbia were fully
developed during this period. They had a large population and they had
developed a social system so impressive that apparently a group of Buddhist priests visiting what is now British Columbia in 458 A.D. called it a

---

5 *Hunting Grounds*
"The hunters of the different numayms can not go hunting on the hunting grounds
of the hunters of another numaym ; for all the hunters own their hunting grounds"
Boas, "Ethnology," 134.
Berry Picking Grounds
"for each numaym owns berry picking grounds for all kinds of berries" *Ibid.*, 135.
Rivers
"The numayms of all the tribes also all own rivers" *Ibid.*, 134.

6 "That is how it happened that they came together. Now they invited one another in
the village Qalogwis and Q!abe and Adap! for they were ready in the villages they
had built." *Ibid.*, 138.

"land well organized." The visit of these Buddhist priests is mentioned by Dr. Robert E. McKechnie in "Strong Medicine."

The earliest voyage on record is a visit by a group of Buddhist priests who were reported to have arrived in the year 458 A.D. In 499 A.D., the last of these priests was reported to have returned to Asia. His name was Hoei-shin (sometimes called Hwai-shan) and his home was Cophene, identified as a town in Afghanistan. His report is incorporated in the official yearbook of the Chinese Empire of that year and in it he describes the Kingdom of Fusang (a region that Captain Cook's charts placed in the vicinity of Vancouver) as a land well organized and ruled by a "king" assisted by his noblemen. It is also recorded that Hoei-shin introduced Buddhism to Fusang.[7]

My grandmother, Daisy Roberts, often told me about stories of strange visitors landing on the west coast of Vancouver Island. The Nəmgis tribe intermarried with the people of the west coast and we have many relatives there. She also mentioned a group of strange-looking men that the Nəmgis met at the headwaters of what is now known as the Nimpkish River. They could not communicate with these men because they could no longer speak. They appeared to be lost and very hungry but they would not come near the Nəmgis who found them. It appeared that some of them had gone mad, and they all ran away never to be seen again.[8]

The Kʷaguł people continued with their way of life, not realizing that across the sea a Queen that they had never heard of was sending a man by the name of Sir Francis Drake to our continent in 1577, 119 years after the Buddhist priests. When he landed he named the area "New Albion." The place where he landed is thought to be in the vicinity of Long Beach on the

---

[7] Robert E. McKechnie, *Strong Medicine* (Vancouver: J. J. Douglas, 1972), 7.

[8] "It seems that about the year 1639 the Japanese government had ordered all junks to be built with open sterns and large square rudders that made them unfit for ocean navigation. It was the government's hope in this way to confine the Japanese to their own islands. In bad weather the unwieldly rudders were soon washed away and the vessels fell into the trough of the sea and rolled their masts out. The Kuro Shiwo current then swept them at a rate of at least ten miles a day northwards toward the Aleutian Islands and then south along the coasts of what were to become Alaska, British Columbia, and the United States. Some junks arrived with a few of their crew members still alive after a drifting voyage that averaged eight to ten months. The longest recorded being seventeen months. The junks were all Japanese and their wrecks, along with miscellaneous flotsam, were often washed up along the western coast of Canada and were the prime source of copper and iron for the natives." *Ibid.*, 172.

"The story of such an accidental voyage is given in the records of the Hudson's Bay Company brig Llama, sent in 1834 to rescue three sailors who had been blown across the Pacific in a junk loaded with crockery of the flower-pot and willow-pattern design and finally wrecked off Cape Flattery. They were taken as slaves by the Indians and, after rescue by Captain McNeal, repatriated by way of England to the Orient." *Ibid.*, 8.

west coast of Vancouver Island. When he landed he claimed the coast for the Queen of England, and this claim was the origin of England's claim to our lands, without consultation or consent of our people. This was to be the beginning of sorrows for the native peoples of British Columbia.[9]

Far across the sea in a place called England, a scene was being played out that was to change the course of history for the North American peoples. The English were to charter a company that was to be used in the future to be the prime adversary of our people. They were to be used to take away our land and our freedom in our own country. Wide-ranging powers were given to the Hudson's Bay Company by the British in 1670. They received sole trading rights in a territory that was to be named Rupert's Land in the Hudson's Bay territories. It was to take a few more years before the Kʷaguɬ nation actually had an encounter with these intruders.

The Indian nations along the coast had no idea that a war had broken out between the British and French in 1756 and that the Algonquin of the eastern woodlands sided with the French and most of the Iroquis supported the British forces. They were also oblivious to the fact that the French were defeated and that when they surrendered they signed the Treaty of Paris on 10 February 1763 ceding almost all their remaining territories in Canada to the British Crown without consulting the allied Indian nations in that region.

They were also oblivious to the fact that a Royal Proclamation was being signed 7 October 1763 at the Court of St. James's by the King of England. If this Royal Proclamation had been adhered to, land claims would not be an issue today. The Royal Proclamation ruled that the governments required that Indian Nations consent before allowing white people to settle in the Indian territories of Canada.

In part it read:

And, We do further strictly enjoin and require all Persons whatever who have either wilfully or inadvertently seated themselves upon any Lands within the Countries above described, or upon any other Lands which, not having been

---

[9] "In conclusion, Bishop remarks that the Government of British Columbia became so convinced that Drake had reached the latitude of Vancouver Island that the highest peak on the Island was named after Drake's ship, *The Golden Hinde*.

The landing that Drake made at the furthermost reach of his voyage is thought to have been in the vicinity of Long Beach on the West Coast of Vancouver Island. It was his naming of the territory as New Albion and his claim of it for his Queen that was the origin of England's claim to the coast. New Albion was shown as English territory on many early charts." Ibid., 175.

ceded to or purchased by us, are still reserved to the said Indians as aforesaid, forthwith to remove themselves from such Settlements.[10]

The native nations along the coast did not know it at the time, but this Royal Proclamation of 1763 was going to play an important part in their lives. Because of its "Indian protection" clause the Royal Proclamation of 1763 prevented the complete annihilation of the Native Nation of Canada.

Captain James Cook landed at Nootka Sound in 1778. The Nəmǧis were frequent visitors to the west coast of Vancouver Island. There was a trail from the headwaters of the Nimpkish Lake to the west coast. It was called the "grease trail," and it was a four-day journey to the village of the Mawičəda?aq̓ at Gold River. The Nəmǧis had intermarried with them for years. The two powerful chiefs of the west coast, Chief Galiǧəmē and Chief Mək̓ʷəla (later to be pronounced Maquinna), had many relatives among the K̓ʷaguł nation. They had obtained their names as a marriage dowry from the Nəmǧis. Mek̓ʷəla means "moon" and Galiǧəmē means "first in rank."

The Nəmǧis had seen first hand how these strangers treated the people of the west coast. The cruelties they endured at the hands of the sailors were to prevent the west coast people from ever wanting to participate in any celebration commemorating the arrival of the Europeans.[11] So when Captain George Vancouver landed at the Nimpkish River on 19 July 1792 this was not the first time the Nəmǧis ever saw the Mamałnē, a name given to these strangers by the people of the west coast which means "people who live on the water." They came, took a few furs, and did not stay.

In 1849 the clan Sənx̌əm was giving a potlatch at Qaluǧʷis, known today as Turnour Island. The twelve clans had formed a confederation of clans under three tribal names, the K̓ʷaguł, the q̓umuyoy̓i, and the Walas K̓ʷaguł. The Sənx̌ē had joined the K̓ʷaguł tribal group. The eleven clans were invited to the potlatch as well as the Mamaliliqəla tribe who lived at Mimk̓ʷəmlis, known today as Village Island. It was during this time that a messenger arrived at the potlatch informing the clans that white people were building a house at their place of descent in what was to be later called Beaver Harbour at Fort Rupert, known today as Port

[10] Cited in A. Shortt and A. Doughty, eds., *Documents Relating to the Constitutional History of Canada, 1759-1791* (2 parts, King's Printer, Ottawa, 1918), part 1, 167.

[11] "The weather was wet and cold and the natives of the area were disturbed at times to the point of violence by these white settlers from another world." McKechnie, *Strong Medicine*, 100.

"when naval manpower was short, it was a case of any able-bodied man would do, and the prisons and other institutions were drained of debtors, felons and madmen to be made into sailors." Ibid., 54.

McNeill. The Chief of the Maʔəmtagila clan, Chief x̌aqʷadᶻi, spoke to the assembled clans:

O mamaleleqala! and you Kwagut ! how do you feel about the white people who have come and built a house at Tsaxis?[12]

Many of the clans did not believe that such a thing was happening because these white strangers would come and pick up a few furs but would never stay for any length of time. So Chief x̌aqʷadᶻi made a suggestion that they should go and see if this was really happening. To their disbelief the messenger was not wrong.

"Let us go and see them!" Thus he said. Immediately all agreed to what he said. Then all the Kwagut and Mamaleleqala and Qǃomoyaye, and the Walus Kwagut went to Tsaxis. Now they believed what was reported to them at Qaloqwis.[13]

The clans did not like what they were seeing. These strangers had moved in and took their land without consent. It was not just any land, but land given to them after the flood. The clans all agreed to move to Fort Rupert to try and protest against these intruders building on their land.

The Kwagut and the Mamaleleqala went back at once to bring their houses and all their property, and they came to build houses at Fort Rupert, Now the Kwagut really left their village sites at Qalogwis, and the Qǃomoyaye their village site at Tsǃade, and the Walus Kʷagut their village site at Adapǃe, and they stayed at Fort Rupert.[14]

They found out very quickly that these strangers were interested in a black stone they called "dᶻəǧʷət". The intruders did not treat them very well. In fact, they acted like they owned the land and the clans were the intruders. A year later the situation got much worse, especially when the English and Scottish miners went on strike against the Hudson's Bay Company. The miners had a contract with the Hudson's Bay Company to mine coal for them at Fort Rupert, but the miners wanted to go to California to mine gold for themselves.[15]

---

[12] Boas, "Ethnology," 97.

[13] Ibid., 96.

[14] *Ibid.*, 97.

[15] "These English coal-miners had hardly settled in before they contributed another "first" to British Columbia's history by going on strike. The spectacle of men actually refusing to do their work after they had accepted employment was a new experience for the H.B.C. For a few days Captain McNeill, in command of the fort, kept the ringleaders shackled and imprisoned in one of its bastions but his action did not end the strike. The men became more militant." G. P. V. and Helen Akrigg, *British Columbia Chronicle 1847-1871* (Vancouver: Discovery Press, 1977), 31-32.

The Mamaliliqəla decided that they did not want anything to do with these intruders that they now referred to as "Mamat?a". They left their village site of Padᶻawa, now known as Thomas Point, and moved back to Mimqəmlis or Village Island, but the other clans remained.

but the Mamaleleqala did not stay long, then they went back to memkumlis; and the Kwaguɫ and Q!omoyoye and Walas Kʷaguɫ and also the Q!omk-!ut!es kept together, and they built at Fort Rupert,[16]

The sudden decline of the native population at Fort Rupert puzzled the agent of the Hudson's Bay Company. The population was very large in number when the Mamaliliqəla were with them, for the Mamaliliqəla and Kʷaguɫ clans were very large in number in 1849. After the Mamalil-iqəla left and moved back to Village Island, the Hudson's Bay agent estimated the remaining population to be ten thousand. Governor Blanshard wrote to Earl Grey about the native population on 5 June 1850:

A Mr. McNeill, agent for the Hudson's Bay Company at Beaver Harbour, who is considered to be better acquainted with the Indian population than any other person, estimates their number at the very largest at ten thousand and these he considers to be steadily decreasing, although the sale of spiritous liquors has been for a considerable time prohibited, and the prohibition appears to be strictly enforced.[17]

The tribes that stayed — the Kʷaguɫ, the q̓umuyoy̓i, and the Walas Kʷaguɫ — were very angry with these intruders. Not only were they building on their land without permission but they were taking resources out of their territory. The situation became so serious that the mine doctor and magistrate of Fort Rupert wrote to Chief Factor Douglas submitting his resignation:

I cannot stop here; nothing but trouble day after day; not a moment's peace or quietness and now to add to our misfortunes, everyone is afraid for his life, and the fort, and not without reason, for certainly there is not a sufficient number to defend it against the large tribe of Indians here, who are becoming very saucy and the men are afraid of them. As far as I could, it has been my endeavor to check and remedy complaints; these have now grown beyond remedy and probably abandoning the fort shortly will be the cure. I was sent here on account of the miners. They have disappeared; so please allow me to do the same in the "Mary Dare."[18]

· When the Kʷaguɫ people realized that these intruders were not going to go away they started trading with them and a better relationship de-

[16] Boas, "Ethnology," 55.

[17] Pethick, *The Fort*, 78.

[18] Akrigg & Akrigg, *British Columbia Chronicle 1847-1871*, 33.

veloped. Dr. Helmcken was to say in later years that the natives in Fort Rupert were "in reality, . . . our best friends and wished to be on good terms with us."[19]

Shortly after this the Kʷaguɫ, the q̓umoyoy̓i, and the Waɫas Kʷaguɫ had a major disagreement that was to change the clan alliances one more time. Chief Maxwa of the Maʔəmtaǥiɫa clan was killed by the Chief of the Kukwək̓əm clan. They both belonged to the Kʷaguɫ tribe.

When they were at Qaɫuǥʷis or Turnour Island, the clans formed three clan confederations: the Kʷaguɫ, the Waɫas Kʷaguɫ, and the q̓umuyoy̓i. After the murder, four clan confederations were formed at Fort Rupert: the Kʷix̌amut, who were once the Kʷaguɫ; the Waɫas Kʷaguɫ; the Kʷix̌a, who were once the q̓umuyoy̓i; and the q̓ʷəmk̓utəs.

The Kʷix̌amut were sometimes called Gʷitəla. After several years these four confederated clans were to become one and were renamed the "Kʷaguɫ".

Many of these clans were to scatter into other clan alliances outside of Fort Rupert after the murder of Chief Maxʷa.

When Maxwa was killed some of the Gexsem went to the Gwetela of the Kwaguɫ. Therefore the Gwetela have Gexsem, and they also went to the Gosgimux. The Gexsem xsanaɫ are Gexsem, and there are also Gexsem of the Naqemǥilisaɫa, and Gexsem of the L!aL!asiqwaɫa, and Gexsem of the Denaxdax, and Gexsem of the Haxwamis, and Gexsem of the Wiwaqe. This is referred to by the old people of the Kwaguɫ as 'blown away by the past Chief Maxwa, when he was killed and also the same happened to the Numayn of the Giǥiɫgam, and they all come from the Numaym of Omaxt-!aɫaɫē. They scattered to all the tribes beginning at the time when Maxwa was killed, for there was only one Numaym Giǥiɫgam of Waɫas Kwaxila-nokume, the father of Omaxt!aɫaɫē.[20]

A few years later a so called "treaty" was signed with the Kʷaguɫ Indians. It is not clear if this "treaty" was signed with the Kʷaguɫ only or with the q̓umuyoy̓i, the Waɫas Kʷaguɫ, and the q̓umk̓utəs. This so-called treaty was signed with an "x". James Douglas claimed he purchased Fort Rupert Indian lands and resources for the equivalent of $3,000 in goods along with other lands in British Columbia. My grandmother, Daisy Roberts, told me that one of the daughters of the Hudson's Bay factor, Robert Hunt, was sent by the Hudson's Bay Company to go door to door with blankets, shirts, and other trade items. She told the people that "Ottawa" was "potlatching." They were asked to put an "x"

---

[19] Loc. cit.
[20] Boas, "Ethnology," 804.

on the paper to signify that they had received their Potlatch gift. For years Kʷakʷala-speaking people thought that Ottawa was a man who ruled over the white people. My grandmother said the native people were shocked when they were ordered out of their property by the Hudson's Bay Company. When they refused, a gun boat was ordered to settle the matter.[21] The reason they gave for the attack was that the clans at Fort Rupert had killed a poor defenceless Haida Chief who just happened to have taken refuge at the fort. The Haida Chief Gedaẋon was indeed killed by the Kʷaguɬ, but the Hudson's Bay neglected to mention that the Chief was related to the Hudson's Bay factor's wife and that that was the reason why he was "visiting" the fort. The clans knew that the navy was called in because they refused to leave what they knew to be their land. They claimed they never sold any land to the Hudson's Bay Company; nor did they know what a treaty was, and to their knowledge had never seen one.

The population of the native Indians was dwindling because of the diseases being brought into the country. The smallpox was the worst, since it was hinted that this was being used to systematically eliminate the first peoples of this country.

When the white people came in the spring, they had sealed Hudson's Bay blankets with them. When they opened them, they handled them with gloves, from here, the smallpox epidemic started. The white people's intention was to kill us all, but we were saved by the great Indian doctors.[22]

On April 20, 1900, at a regular meeting of the Victoria Medical Society, Doctor Dave was to state:

The first epidemic of smallpox occurred in 1862 when the Indians suffered principally from its ravages. In those days they died like rats and their bodies could be seen lying around Ogden Point by the fifties.[23]

Many of the native people tried to go to Victoria thinking that they would get help from the white doctors, but they were forced to return to their villages spreading the dreaded disease up and down the coast.

[21] The capital city of Victoria was far from the mainland Indian territories. White racists there suggested Canada's treaty-making policy was "your new fangled system of timely precaution, friendly conversation as between men with equal rights and gentle treatment, and equitable principles [which] may suit the atmosphere of Ottawa, but it won't do for our Siwashes. . . ." They preferred genocide to making treaties. "If Indians complain, send a gunboat to them; we have gunboated them for twenty years." Joanne Drake-Terry, *The Same as Yesterday*, (Lillooet: Lillooet Tribal Council, 1989), 107.

[22] Ibid., 85.

[23] T. E. Rose, M.D., *From Shaman to Modern Medicine* (Vancouver: Mitchell Press, 1972), 129.

Smallpox broke out among the northern Indian people living in Victoria in May. The police torched their living quarters and sent the sick and dying packing.[24]

When they reached their villages, the native people tried to isolate themselves to protect their own people from catching this dreaded disease. As a Lieutenant Palmer wrote about the Bella Coolas:

Poor creatures, they are dying and rotting away by the score, it is no uncommon occurrence to come across dead bodies lying in the bush. They have now dispersed from the villages, but it seems to be spreading through the valley.[25]

While the native people were dying of the smallpox all over British Columbia, the government was wasting no time in trying to find ways of taking more land. James Douglas retired as Commissioner of Lands and Works in 1863, and he recommended that Joseph William Trutch take his place. Trutch felt that the native Indians were an inferior race. He was to say: "the idiosyncrasy of the Indians in this country appears to incapacitate them from appreciating any abstract idea."[26] Trutch's answer to dealing with the Indians was to use military force.

After he was appointed Chief Commissioner of Lands and Works, the wholesale give-away of Indian lands and resources flourished. Trutch thought it morally appropriate to use military force to deal with Indian Nations' resistance to the illegal takeover of their lands and resources. Trutch resolved to prevent the Indian nations from owning or retaining any lands whatsoever in the British Colonies.[27]

The Dominion of Kanata (Huron-Iroquis for "Indian village or settlement") was formed in 1867. It consisted of the four provinces of Ontario, Quebec, Nova Scotia, and New Brunswick. Britain, by means of the British North America Act (BNA Act), reorganized these colonies, and the Dominion of Canada was born.

Under section 91(24) of the Act, the new Canadian Parliament at Ottawa claimed legislative authority over "Indians and lands reserved for Indians." Under this section the Canadian government was obliged to honour the commitments the Crown had made to the Indian nations in the Royal Proclamation of 1763.

The 109th section of the BNA Act put the Indian territories of Ontario, Quebec, Nova Scotia, and New Brunswick under the jurisdiction of these provincial governments. Britain had made treaties with the Indian nations

---

[24] Drake-Terry, *The Same as Yesterday*, 85.
[25] Akrigg & Akrigg, *British Columbia Chronicle 1847-1871*, 253.
[26] Drake-Terry, *The Same as Yesterday*, 100.
[27] Ibid., 96.

of these provinces. They could prove it was legitimately acquired and that they had followed the terms of the Royal Proclamation of 1763 concerning how "unceded" land was to be obtained.

On 20 July 1871 British Columbia joined the Dominion of Canada. Lientenant-Governor Trutch (the previous Commissioner of Lands and Works) and his provincial legislature decided that the 109th section of the 1867 BNA Act could be interpreted to mean that all unceded Indian lands and resources were "public" lands which were "automatically" placed under the control of British Columbia upon confederation with Canada. The provincial government stated that the provincial legislature did not have to recognize Indian title or negotiate treaties with the Indian nations in British Columbia. On several occasions Ottawa told the provincial legis-lature of British Columbia that this was not "legal." The first session of the provincial legislature also passed an Act denying Indian people the right to vote or hold public office.

The provincial government knew that its assumption of the "automatic" transfer of Indian lands was not legal, so it passed a "land act" on 2 March 1874. This treated all unceded Indian land as being under a grant from the British Crown and so allowed the provincial government to control and dispose of Indian lands and resources. No such grant had, however, ever been issued because it would have failed to follow the Royal Proclamation of 1763, which clearly stated that "any other lands not having been ceded to or purchased by us, are still reserved to the said Indians." It was also clear that the only way lands could be ceded was through a treaty with the Indian nations of British Columbia.

Ten months after the land act was passed, Justice Minister T. Fournier, in Ottawa, submitted a legal opinion on the legality of the Act to the Dominion government and to Lord Dufferin, the Governor-General of Canada. He reminded them of the contents of the Royal Proclamation of 1763, "that the Indians should not be molested." His legal opinion of the Act was not what they wanted to hear.

Considering then . . . that no surrender or cessions of their territorial rights . . . [have] been ever executed by the Indian tribes of the province the under-signed feels he cannot do otherwise than advise that the Act . . . is objection-able as tending to deal with lands which are assumed to be absolute property of the province, an assumption which completely ignores as applicable to the Indians of British Columbia, the honor and good faith with which the Crown has, in all other cases, since its sovereignty of the territories in North America, dealt with their various Indian tribes.[28]

28 Ibid., 115.

Lieutenant-Governor Trutch did not want treaties to be made with the Indian nations. He warned the federal and provincial governments to avoid doing so.

If you now commence to buy out Indian title to the lands of British Columbia you would go back on all that has been done for thirty years past and would be equitably bound to compensate tribes who inhabited districts now settled and farmed by white people, equally with those in the more remote and uncultivated portions.[29]

Prime Minister Mackenzie and his cabinet were afraid that British Columbia might renounce Confederation, so they would not disallow the Land Act. They solved their problem by legislating the "Indian Act" of 1876, placing all Indians in Canada under wardship. This stopped all direct conveyance of land to the native people. It also made native Indians on reserves second-class people. They could not vote or receive any pensions, in time family allowances were denied them, and they were not considered citizens of the province of British Columbia or of Canada. On 1 January 1884 a special law prohibiting potlatches in the Indian territories of British Columbia was added to the Indian Act. This was later repealed in 1951.

The native Indians were finally granted full citizenship rights in 1960. In the Hansard of 18 January 1960, the speech of Prime Minister John Diefenbaker was reported:

The other measure, the provision to give Indians the vote, is one of those steps which will have an effect everywhere in the world — for the reason that wherever I went last year on the occasion of my trip to commonwealth countries, it was brought to my atention that in Canada the original people within our country excepting for a qualified class, were denied the right to vote. I say that so far as this long overdue measure is concerned, it will remove everywhere in the world any suggestion that colour or race places any citizen in our country in a lower category than the other citizens of our country.[30]

When the native Indians were given Canadian citizenship, the President of the Native Brotherhood of British Columbia called it "a wonderful victory."

Granting of the federal vote to Native Indians is indeed a wonderful victory. Today we have cause to be proud of the great fight the Native Brotherhood of British Columbia has conducted over the years. And we should humbly give thanks to God for sustaining us in our struggle to win better conditions and equality of citizenship and education for the Native people.

[29] Ibid., 121.

[30] *Native Voice*, Special Edition, 1960, 3. "Native Indians Granted Full Citizenship Rights."

After years of "wardship", years of hardship and suffering caused by the neglect and indifference of white governments to those who were first in the land, Native Indians at last stand as full citizens.

I am proud of my people, proud of what the Native Brotherhood has accomplished and confident that out of their splendid heritage the Native Indians will make an ever greater contribution to the progress of their country.[31]

But nothing had really changed, for we were still under wardship and the "promise" to settle land claims did not materialize. British Columbia negotiated to join Confederation and become part of Canada and then made sure we were legislated "out."

It is now 1991, and native Indians in British Columbia are still trying to get the provincial and federal governments to settle with them for their land and resources. Treaties were made with the Indian nations of Ontario, Quebec, Nova Scotia, and New Brunswick. The Indian nations under the treaty were guaranteed lands and certain rights. As I watch the news I see the Mohawks in Oka, Quebec defending the very land that was included in this treaty because the white population wanted to build a golf course on their land. I wondered about the clause in the Royal Proclamation of 1763 stating "that the Indians should not be molested," when the provincial and federal governments called in the army. As I watched, my mind flashed back to the prophetic words of the *Mainland Colony* newspaper of 11 May 1864.

We are quite aware that there are those amongst us who are disposed to ignore altogether the rights of the Indians and their claims upon us ... depend on it, for every acre of land we obtain by improper means we will have to pay for dearly in the end. ...[32]

[31] Loc. cit.

[32] Drake-Terry, *The Same as Yesterday*, 88.

Use of International Phonetic Alphabet by Native Groups

The International Phonetic Alphabet (IPA) is an alphabet that has been used internationally for years by different language groups around the world. It has over 100 characters and it is said that if you learn all the characters you will be able to write most of the world's languages.

The Liq̓ʷala/Kʷak̓ʷala language uses forty-eight of these characters. The language programme in Campbell River was started by the University of Victoria, where this particular orthography is taught. Several native groups have chosen this particular orthography because it has characters for all the sounds in their particular language grouping.

The Liq̓ʷala/Kʷak̓ʷala language is being taught at the Carihi Secondary School in Campbell River as a second language unit. The students are taught the grammar and sentence structure of the language and they are taught to speak, read, and write in the Liq̓ʷala/Kʷak̓ʷala language using the IPA.

a	b	c	c̓	d	d^{z}	ē	e	ə	g
gʷ	ǧ	ǧʷ	h	i	k	k̓	kʷ	k̓ʷ	l
i̓	ł	λ	ƛ	ƛ̓	m	m̓	n	n̓	o
p	p̓	q	qʷ	q̓	q̓ʷ	s	t	t̓	u
w	w̓	x	xʷ	x̌	x̌ʷ	y	y̓	ʔ	

VOWELS

ENGLISH VOWELS	Liq̓ʷala/Kʷak̓ʷala VOWELS	Liq̓ʷala/Kʷak̓ʷala SOUNDS
A	A	AAH
E	E	EH
I	I	EE
O	O	OH
U	U	OOO
	ə "shwa"	UUH
Y (sometimes)	ē (sometimes)	A

The Alphabet with Pictures

a ʔayasu	**b** babagʷəm	**c** cupáli	**c'** camaci	**d** dəmalē (L) dəlaxē (K)	**d^z** dᵃoli
ē həmaʔelas	**e** ʔeǧas	**ə** ʔom/ʔe	**g** gukʷ	**gʷ** gʷəsu	**ǧ** ǧadᵃoq
ǧʷ ǧʷoyəm	**h** hawax̌ayu	**i** ʔipa	**k** kəx̌əlaǧa	**k'** k'adayu	**kʷ** kʷikʷ
k'ʷ k'ʷisa	**l** ləqʷa	**l'** l'astu	**ł** łaxʷəmala	**λ** λabəm	**ƛ** ƛaqəla
ƛ' ƛ'isəla	**m** mayus	**m'** m'əkʷəla	**n** nəx̌aq	**n'** n'əm	**o** ʔogiwē
p puxʷons	**p'** p'əsp'ayu	**q** qos (L) kʷusi (K)	**qʷ** qʷəx̌	**q'** q'osʔanē	**q'ʷ** q'ʷasa
s siłəm	**t** tominas	**t'** t'ibayu	**u** ʔupigē ʔukʷexē	**w** wəqes	**w'** w'aci
x xoldayu	**xʷ** xʷeyu	**x̌** x̌aq	**x̌ʷ** x̌ʷənukʷ	**y** yawapsoms	**y'** y'ugʷa

From A Bridge

So many straight and angular buildings
Stand on true square streets,
Defining equal length blocks.
Attempts at absolute, complete, control.

At the top of the hill authority reigns;
A tower and steeples jutting, rise.
The tiny red leaf announces to all,
"The government is in session."

Across the river, and low,
Married to its graceful banks.
The curvaceous one reposes,
Opposite and opposed as well.

Here the pavement simply wanders,
And draws one to the building,
That follows the contours of the land,
And pays homage to creation.

Winter 1988,
on the Interprovincial
Bridge, Ottawa-Hull,
for Douglas Cardinal

Conspiracy of Legislation:
The Suppression of Indian Rights in Canada

CHIEF JOE MATHIAS and GARY R. YABSLEY

"Without question, this legislation struck at the heart of what was most sacred to West Coast Indian societies. In so doing, it put in question the very survival of these nations."

JOE MATHIAS, whose Indian name is St'sūkwanem, is a hereditary Chief of the Squamish people. He has also held the position of elected Chief since 1967 when he won it by acclamation. In 1969 he was appointed by his people as the political spokesperson for the Squamish nation. For seventeen years he worked as the band's housing administrator, and in 1985 he became the Land Claims Coordinator. In the same year he was selected by other British Columbia bands as British Columbia's regional vice-president to the Assembly of First Nations. He was re-elected by acclamation in 1988 and resigned the post in 1990. At the British Columbia regional level he has been active with the Aboriginal Council, the First Nations Congress and various organizations dealing with fisheries issues. Nationally, Joe has worked on the constitution and the Cooligan report on the federal land claims policy.

Gary Yabsley is an associate in the law firm of Ratcliff & Co. in North Vancouver. He has represented Indian & Inuit nations on a broad range of matters for over fifteen years, during which time he and Chief Mathias co-authored this article. Gary is currently completing his doctorate in political science at the University of Texas in Austin, Texas.

* * *

The recent escalation of aboriginal rights issues and litigation in British Columbia has prompted an oft-repeated argument from those who oppose the recognition of any Indian interest in land in this province. This argument basically asserts that First Nations did nothing over the past century to protect their rights and should therefore be barred at this late date from claiming those rights. Indians have, the argument goes, "slept on their rights."

In truth, the Indian assertion of aboriginal title has never ceased. The historical record is clear on this fact. This persistence has characterized Indian relations in this province despite an array of federal and provincial legislation specifically designed to eliminate Indian rights by denying them access to both legal and political institutions. Upon examination, these laws can be seen to be the root cause of much of the injustice and inequity that continues to permeate the Indian presence in Canada. By any just standard these laws are offensive.

The consequences of this legislation in terms of the loss of economic well-being, political power, cultural integrity and spiritual strength are immeasurable. We know with certainty that these laws deprived First Nations of their material wealth by denying them access to their traditional lands and resources. Further, we know that these laws prohibited Indian governments from exercising any real power in the political and legal systems. And we know that extensive legislation was passed, the sole purpose of which was to destroy the Indian identity and Indian values in Canada.

From an Indian perspective, this legislation represents nothing less than a conspiracy. Examined as a whole, it exhibits a clear pattern founded on a conscious intent to eliminate Indians and "indianness" from Canadian society.

What exactly did this legislation do? For one thing, it struck a crippling blow to the Indian relationship to their lands. In an effort to encourage European immigration, the colonial and provincial governments pursued a policy of land pre-emptions or grants. In essence, any European male over the age of eighteen could simply occupy 320 acres of land and ultimately claim legal title to it. This could be done regardless of any pre-existing Indian rights to these lands. No compensation was ever paid for this loss.

Moreover, the same legislation specifically prohibited any Indian from claiming a right of pre-emption. Thus, the Colonial Land Ordinance of 1870, for example, stated in section 3:

3. From and after the date of proclamation in this Colony of Her Majesty's assent to this Ordinance, any male person being a British Subject, of the age of eighteen years or over, may acquire the right to pre-empt any tract of unoccupied, unsurveyed, and unreserved Crown Lands (not being an Indian settlement) not exceeding three hundred and twenty acres in extent in that portion of the Colony situate to the northward and eastward of the Cascade or Coast Range of Mountains, and one hundred and sixty acres in extent in the rest of the Colony. Provided that such right of pre-emption shall not be held to extend to any of the Aborigines of this Continent, except to such as shall have obtained the Governor's special permission in writing to that effect.

This impairment of Indian land rights was compounded by federal legislation that denied First Nations access to the courts. In 1927, the federal government amended the Indian Act to make it illegal for an Indian or Indian nation to retain a lawyer to advance their claims, or even to raise money with the intention of retaining a lawyer. Anyone convicted of this offence could be imprisoned.

Section 141 of the 1927 Indian Act stated:

141. Every person who, without the consent of the Superintendent General expressed in writing, receives, obtains, solicits or requests from an Indian any

payment or contribution or promise of any payment or contribution for the purpose of raising a fund or providing money for the prosecution of any claim which the tribe or band of Indians to which such Indian belongs, or of which he is a member, has or is represented to have for the recovery of any claim or money for the benefit of the said tribe or band, shall be guilty of an offence and liable upon summary conviction for each such offence to a penalty not exceeding two hundred dollars and not less than fifty dollars or to imprisonment for any term not exceeding two months.

Indian nations were therefore denied those fundamental rights that are taken for granted in any democratic system. They were, as a matter of colonial and provincial policy, denied rights to lands they had occupied for centuries. This exclusion from the land was extended through the discriminatory provisions of colonial and provincial land legislation. And they were prohibited by federal law seeking a legal remedy for this injustice.

The federal government played an instrumental role in other parts of the country in severing the ties between Indians and their lands. The Indian Act of 1876, for instance, prohibited Indians from acquiring or pre-empting lands in Manitoba or the Northwest Territories. Section 70 of that Act provides that:

70. No Indian or non-treaty Indian, resident in the province of Manitoba, the North-West Territories or the territory of Keewatin, shall be held capable of having acquired or acquiring a homestead or pre-emption right to a quarter section, or any portion of land in any surveyed or unsurveyed lands in the said province of Manitoba, the North-West Territories or the territory of Keewatin, or the right to share in the distribution of any lands allotted to half-breeds, subject to the following exceptions: ...

It is also worthy of note that after the McKenna-McBride Commission attempted to resolve questions about the nature and extent of Indian reserves in British Columbia in 1916, the federal and provincial governments passed legislation removing extensive tracts of valuable land from many reserves in the province. This was done without the approval of the First Nations and, indeed, was contrary to the express provisions of the Indian Act that required a surrender in order to alienate any reserve lands. Until recently, no compensation was paid for the loss of these lands.

The economic consequences of the loss of lands and resources is easy to appreciate. What is less obvious is the extent to which federal law in particular reached into Indian communities in an effort to suffocate the most forceful elements of traditional Indian political life and cultural identity. The Indian Act was repeatedly used to destroy traditional institutions of Indian government and to abolish those cultural practices that defined Indian identity.

For British Columbia First Nations, this assault focused on the potlatch and practices of the longhouse. Traditionally, the longhouse was the centre of Indian government and the spiritual focal point of an Indian community. All things of community importance took place in the longhouse: the passing of laws, the giving of names, spiritual dancing, funerals, and more. The potlatch was, and is, the most fundamental ceremony to take place in the longhouse. Elaborate and complex, the potlatch, through its ritual, reinforces the value systems upon which Indian societies have defined themselves for centuries.

Yet from 1880 to 1951, the Indian Act outlawed the potlatch and sacred dancing. Section 3 of the Indian Act of 1880, for example, provides that:

3. Every Indian or other person who engages in or assists in celebrating the Indian festival known as the "Potlatch" or in the Indian dance known as the "Tamanawas" is guilty of a misdemeanour, and shall be liable to imprisonment for a term of not more than six nor less than two months in any gaol or other place of confinement; and any Indian or other person who encourages, directly or indirectly, an Indian or Indians to get up such a festival or dance, or to celebrate the same, or who shall assist in the celebration of the same is guilty of a like offence, and shall be liable to the same punishment.

The 1927 Indian Act was even more extensive in its prohibition and in its efforts to increase the powers of federal officials over the lives of Indian people. Section 140 of this Act states that:

140(1) Every Indian or other person who engages in, or assists in celebrating or encourages either directly or indirectly another to celebrate any Indian festival, dance or other ceremony of which the giving away or paying or giving back of money, goods or articles of any sort forms a part, or is a feature, whether such gift of money, goods or articles takes place before, at, or after the celebration of the same, or who engages or assists in any celebration or dance of which the wounding or mutilation of the dead or living body of any human being or animal forms a part or is a feature, is guilty of an offence and is liable on summary conviction to imprisonment for a term not exceeding six months and not less than two months.
(2) Nothing in this section shall be construed to prevent the holding of any agricultural show or exhibition or the giving of prizes for exhibits thereat.
(3) Any Indian in the province of Manitoba, Saskatchewan, Alberta or British Columbia, or in the Territories who participates in any Indian dance outside the bounds of his own reserve, or who participates in any show, exhibition, performance, stampede or pageant in aboriginal costume without the consent of the Superintendent General or his authorized agent, and any person who induces or employs any Indian to take part in such dance, show, exhibition, performance, stampede or pageant, or induces any Indian to leave his reserve or employs any Indian for such a purpose, whether the dance, show, exhibition, stampede or pageant has taken place or not, shall on summary

conviction be liable to a penalty not exceeding twenty-five dollars, or to imprisonment for one month, or to both penalty and imprisonment.

In order to avoid the criminal implications of seeking to preserve their traditional political power, and to follow their own religious beliefs, Indian communities were forced to take the potlatch to secluded places beyond the reach of the RCMP. On more than one occasion, elders were arrested, and even imprisoned, for participating in a potlatch. Without question, this legislation struck at the heart of what was most sacred to West Coast Indian societies. In so doing, it put in question the very survival of these nations.

Having outlawed the political institutions and traditional form of Indian government, the federal government proceeded to superimpose its own form of government on Indian nations. The band council system was introduced through the Indian Act and functioned on European perceptions of what constituted proper government. It was a system of government that had little meaning in Indian communities. Moreover, band councils were left with little or no ability to control the destiny of Indian political affairs. The jurisdiction of band councils was superficial. No substantive powers rested with these councils, and any decisions made were subject to the ultimate approval of the Minister of Indian Affairs.

Stripped of independent political power, Indian nations were then denied access to the political institutions of non-Indian governments. Both federal and provincial legislation operated to deny Indians the right to participate in the politics of the nation. In effect, no Indian voice could be heard in the debates of Parliament or the Legislative Assembly because Indians were prohibited from voting. Every federal Elections Act up to and including the Canada Elections Act of 1952 specifically disqualified Indians from voting.

At the provincial level, Municipal Elections Acts up to and including the Municipal Election Act of 1948 and the provincial Elections Acts up to 1949 prohibited Indians (as well as Chinese and Japanese) from voting. Lacking the right or the capacity to participate in the democratic processes of the nation, one begins to appreciate the full extent of the political debilitation of this legislation. Indian nations were denied the right and the means to function with any degree of independence or self-reliance and, at the same time, were prohibited from functioning in the larger society with the rights and powers enjoyed by non-Indians.

The government's answer to this dilemma was assimilation. Indians were encouraged to give up their aspirations to remain distinct peoples. Both policy and legislation sought to persuade Indians to take on the ways of the white man, in essence, to cease to aspire for the return of their lands or the protection of their cultures and their heritage. The weight of government was brought upon Indians to assimilate.

To this end, Indian children were taken from their homes and placed in residential schools. In these institutions, young children were severed from their families and their cultural values. They were beaten for speaking their own languages or for attempting to practise their own ways. They were made to feel shame for their indianness. They were forcefully encouraged to become white. Any Indian child refusing to attend a federally run residential school was prohibited from attending a provincial school near his or her own community.

The desire of the non-Indian society to force assimilation on Indians is perhaps best expressed in section 99(1) of the Indian Act of 1880. This section provides for the enfranchisement of any Indian obtaining a university degree or becoming a lawyer, priest or minister. In addition, an Indian so enfranchised could be rewarded by the Superintendent-General of Indian Affairs with a grant of land from the reserve lands of the band. The implications of this legislation are clear. Any Indian aspiring to an advanced education was confronted with the loss of his or her Indian identity and Indian status. The message was simple: "We will reward you with Indian land if you give up your Indian ways."

Finally, it is important to appreciate that Indian governments were denied the power to determine how they would allocate their own monies and resources. Indian Acts from 1880 until the present have continually vested in the Governor-in-Council the power to determine if band councils are spending Indian money in an appropriate manner. The Indian Act of 1880, for instance, states in section 70 that:

70. The Governor in Council may, subject to the provisions of this Act, direct how, and in what manner, and by whom, the moneys arising from sales of Indian lands, and from the property held or to be held in trust for the Indians, or from any timber on Indian lands or reserves, or from any other source, for the benefit of Indians, (with the exception of any sum not exceeding ten per cent of the proceeds of any lands, timber or property, which is agreed at the time of the surrender to be paid to the members of the band interested therein,) shall be invested, from time to time, and how the payments or assistance to which the Indians are entitled shall be made or given, — and may provide for the general management of such moneys, and direct what percentage or proportion thereof shall be set apart, from time to time, to cover the cost of and incidental to the management of reserves, lands, property and moneys under the provisions of this Act, and for the construction or repair of roads passing through such reserves or lands, and by way of contribution to schools attended by such Indians.

It is clear from this examination that the federal and provincial legislation over the past one hundred years has impaired and restricted First Nations in every conceivable manner. It has worked not for the betterment of Indian societies but for the elimination of these societies as distinct and vital social orders within Canada. The fact that First Nations continue to exist — indeed, that they forcefully continue to assert their indianness — is testament to the tenacity and strength of these nations. If history has taught us anything, it is that the rest of Canada should be embracing and encouraging these unique identities and values.

*   *   *

APPENDIX

Federal and Provincial Legislation Restricting and Denying Indian Rights

I. PROHIBITION ON RAISING MONEY AND PROSECUTING CLAIMS TO LAND OR RETAINING A LAWYER

A. *Federal Legislation*

i. Indian Act, R.S.C. 1927, s. 141.

141. Every person who, without the consent of the Superintendent General expressed in writing, receives, obtains, solicits or requests from an Indian any payment or contribution for the purpose of raising a fund or providing money for the prosecution of any claim which the tribe or band of Indians to which such Indian belongs, or of which he is a member, has or is represented to have for the recovery of any claim or money for the benefit of the said tribe or band, shall be guilty of an offence and liable upon summary conviction for each such offence to a penalty not exceeding two hundred dollars and not less than fifty dollars or to imprisonment for any term not exceeding two months.

2. PROHIBITION OF RELIGIOUS CEREMONIES AND POTLATCHES

A. *Federal Legislation*

i. Indian Act, 1880 as amended, S.C. 1884, C. 27 (47 Vict.) s. 3.

3. Every Indian or other person who engages in or assists in celebrating the Indian festival known as the "Potlatch" or in the Indian dance known as the "Tamanawas" is guilty of a misdemeanour, and shall be liable to imprisonment for a term of not more than six nor less than two months in any gaol or other place of confinement; and any Indian or other person who encourages, directly or indirectly, an Indian or Indians to get up such a

festival or dance, or to celebrate the same, or who shall assist in the celebration of the same is guilty of a like offence, and shall be liable to the same punishment.

ii. Indian Act, 1886, s. 114 (amended S.C. 1895, C. 35, s. 6).

iii. Indian Act, R.S.C. 1906, C. 81, s. 149.

iv. Indian Act, R.S.C. 1927, C. 98, s. 140.

140(1). Every Indian or other person who engages in, or assists in celebrating or encourages either directly or indirectly another to celebrate any Indian festival, dance or other ceremony of which the giving away or paying or giving back of money, goods or articles of any sort forms a part, or is a feature, whether such gift of money, goods or articles takes place before, at, or after the celebration of the same, or who engages or assists in any celebration or dance of which the wounding or mutilation of the dead or living body of any human being or animal forms a part or is a feature, is guilty of an offence and is liable on summary conviction to imprisonment for a term not exceeding six months and not less than two months.

(2). Nothing in this section shall be construed to prevent the holding of any agricultural show or exhibition or the giving of prizes for exhibits thereat.

(3). Any Indian in the province of Manitoba, Saskatchewan, Alberta, or British Columbia, or in the Territories who participates in any Indian dance outside the bounds of his own reserve, or who participates in any show, exhibition, performance, stampede or pageant in aboriginal costume without the consent of the Superintendent General or his authorized agent, and any person who induces or employs any Indian to take part in such dance, show, exhibition, performance, stampede or pageant, or induces any Indian to leave his reserve or employs any Indian for such a purpose, whether the dance, show, exhibition, stampede or pageant has taken place or not, shall on summary conviction be liable to a penalty not exceeding twenty-five dollars, or to imprisonment for one month, or to both penalty and imprisonment.

3. PROHIBITION AND RESTRICTION ON ACCESS TO FUNDS

A. *Federal Legislation*

i. Indian Act, S.C. 1880, C. 28, s. 70.

70. The Governor in Council may, subject to the provisions of this Act, direct how, and in what manner, and by whom the moneys arising from sales of Indian lands, and from the property held or to be held in trust for the Indians, or from any timber on Indian lands or reserves, or from any other source, for the benefit of Indians, (with the exception of any sum not exceeding ten per cent of the proceeds of any lands, timber or property, which is agreed at the time of the surrender to be paid to the members of

the band interested therein,) shall be invested from time to time, and how the payments or assistance to which the Indians are entitled shall be made or given, — and may provide for the general management of such moneys, and direct what percentage or proportion thereof shall be set apart, from time to time, to cover the cost of and incidental to the management of reserves, lands, property and moneys under the provisions of this Act, and for the construction or repair of roads passing through such reserves or lands, and by way of contribution to schools attended by such Indians.

ii. Indian Act, R.S.C. 1886, C. 43, s. 70 (amended S.C. 1906, C. 20, s. 1).

iii. Indian Act, R.S.C. 1906, C. 81, s. 89.

iv. Indian Act, R.S.C. 1927, C. 98, s. 92.

v. Indian Act, R. S. C. 1952, C. 149, s. 61.

vi. Indian Act, R.S.C. 1970, C. I-6, s. 61.

61.(1) Indian moneys shall be expended only for the benefit of the Indians or bands for whose use and benefit in common the moneys are received or held, and subject to this Act and to the terms of any treaty or surrender, the Governor in Council may determine whether any purpose for which Indian moneys are used or are to be used is for the use and benefit of the band.

4. PROHIBITION ON ACQUIRING LAND

A. *Federal Legislation*

i. Indian Act, S.C. 1876, C. 18, s. 70 (re Manitoba and N.W.T.).

70. No Indian or non-treaty Indian, resident in the province of Manitoba, the North-West Territories or the territory of Keewatin, shall be held capable of having acquired or acquiring a homestead or pre-emption right to a quarter section, or any portion of land in any surveyed or unsurveyed lands in the said province of Manitoba, the North-West Territories or the territory of Keewatin, or the right to share in the distribution of any lands allotted to half-breeds, subject to the following exceptions: . . .

ii. Indian Act, S.C. 1880, C. 20, s. 81.

iii. McKenna-McBride Agreement — 1919 legislation, without surrender.

B. *Colonial and Provincial Legislation*

i. 1861 and 1870 right to pre-emption of lands open only to British subjects; exempted only reserves and settlements.

ii. Land Ordinance, 1870 R.S.B.C. 1871, C. 144, s. 3.

3. From and after the date of the proclamation in this Colony of Her Majesty's assent to this Ordinance, any male person being a British subject, of the age of eighteen years or over, may acquire the right to pre-empt any

tract of unoccupied, unsurveyed, and unreserved Crown Lands (not being an Indian settlement) not exceeding three hundred and twenty acres in extent in that portion of the Colony situate to the northward and eastward of the Cascade or Coast Range of Mountains, and one hundred and sixty acres in extent in the rest of the Colony. Provided that such right of pre-emption shall not be held to extend to any of the Aborigines of this Continent, except to such as shall have obtained the Governor's special permission in writing to that effect.

iii. Land Ordinance Amendment Act, 1873, R.S.B.C. 1873, C. 1.

iv. Land Act, S.B.C. 1874, C. 2, s. 3, s. 24, s. 11.

v. Land Act, S.B.C. 1875, C. 5, s. 3, s. 24, s. 11.

vi. Land Act, S.B.C. 1887, C. 16, s. 3, s. 11.

vii. Land Act, R.S.B.C. 1888, C. 66, s. 14.

14. The occupation of this Act shall mean a continuous bona fide personal residence of the pre-emptor, his agent, or family, on land recorded by such settler; but Indians or Chinamen shall not be considered agents.

viii. Land Act Amendment Act, S.B.C. 1892, C. 24, s. 1; S.B.C. 1893, C. 22, s. 2.

It is to be noted that all of these Lands Acts prohibited pre-emptions of lands by Indians.

5. PROHIBITION ON VOTING RIGHTS

A. *Federal Legislation*

i. Electoral Franchise Act, S.C. 1885, C. 41, s. 11, s. 64.

ii. Electoral Franchise Act, S.C. 1886, C. 5, s. 9, s. 42.

iii. Electoral Franchise Act, S.C. 1890, C. 8, s. 9.

iv. Dominion Bi-Election Act, S.C. 1919, C. 48, s. 5.

v. Dominion Elections Act, S.C. 1920, C. 46, s. 29.

vi. Act to Amend Elections Act, S.C. 1929, C. 40, s. 29.

vii. Dominion Franchise Act, S.C. 1934, C. 51, s. 4.

viii. Dominion Elections Act, S.C. 1938, C. 46, s. 14 as amended.

ix. Act to Amend Dominion Elections Act, S.C. 1951, C. 3, s. 6.

x. Canada Elections Act, R.S.C. 1952, C. 23, s. 14.

14.(2) The following persons are disqualified from voting at an election and incapable of being registered as electors and shall not vote nor be so registered, that is to say,

44

(e) every Indian, as defined in the *Indian Act*, ordinarily resident on a reserve, unless,

(i) he was a member of His Majesty's Forces during World War I or World War II, or was a member of the Canadian Forces who served on active service subsequent to the 9th day of September, 1950, or

(ii) he executed a waiver, in a form prescribed by the Minister of Citizenship and Immigration, of exemptions under the *Indian Act* from taxation on and in respect of personal property, and subsequent to the execution of such waiver a writ has issued ordering an election in any electoral district;

It is to be noted that all of these Elections Acts prohibited Indians from voting. This prohibition was finally repealed in 1960.

B. *Provincial Legislation*

i. Municipal Elections Acts up to 1949 prohibited Indians from voting.

Municipal Elections Act, R.S.B.C. 1948, s. 4:

4. No Chinese, Japanese, or Indians shall be entitled to vote at any municipal election for the election of a Mayor, Reeve, Alderman, or Councillor.

ii. Provincial Elections Acts up to 1949 prohibited Indians from voting.

Provincial Elections Act, R.S.B.C. 1948, s. 4.

4.(1) The following persons shall be disqualified from voting at any election, and shall not make application to have their names inserted in any list of voters:—

(a) Every Indian: Provided that the provisions of this clause shall not disqualify or render incompetent to vote any person who:—

(i) Has served in the Naval, Military, or Air Force of any member of the British Commonwealth of Nations in any war, and who produces a discharge from such Naval, Military, or Air Force to the Registrar upon applying for registration under this Act and to the Deputy Returning Officer at the time of polling:

(ii) Has been enfranchised under the provisions of the "Indian Act" of the Dominion:

(iii) Is not resident upon or within the confines of an Indian reserve:

6. PROHIBITION ON OBTAINING ADVANCED EDUCATION, AUTOMATIC ENFRANCHISEMENT

A. *Federal Legislation*

i. Indian Act, S.C. 1880, C. 28, s. 99(1).

99.(1) Any Indian who may be admitted to the degree of Doctor of Medicine, or to any other degree by any University of Learning, or who may be admitted in any Province of the Dominion to practice law either as an Advocate or as a Barrister or Counsellor, or Solicitor or Attorney or to be a Notary Public, or who may enter Holy Orders, or who may be licensed by any denomination of Christians as a Minister of the Gospel, may, upon petition to the Superintendent-General, ipso facto become and be enfranchised under the provisions of this Act; and the Superintendent-General may give him a suitable allotment of land from the lands belonging to the band of which he is a member.

ii. Indian Act Amended, S.C. 1884, C. 27, s. 16.

B. *Provincial Legislation*

i. Public Schools Acts up to and including the Act of 1948.

92.(4) Chinese, Japanese, and Indians shall not be entitled to vote at any school meeting.

Paper Garrotes

Your promises are remembered
By paper,
Signed.
They are not of the heart,
Remembered by you.

Royal proclamations,
Laws, policies,
Treaties, reserves,
The Indian Act.

All said to be for our protection
"For the exclusive use and benefit of . . ."
Your paper words are violent,
The vulgar weapons of your undeclared war.

Double edged swords,
Your paper promises,
Confined us to little rocky plots,
And gave a country to you.
They built prisons for our children,
And gave privileges to yours.

Your Minister of Indian Affairs,
His special assistants, their consultants,
Secretaries,
They're all experts on Indian Affairs.

The Indian Act
Gives them a voice in our affairs,
And it strangles many of our voices.
Your government's paper garrote tightens

Canada, the mother/fatherland
Of countless immigrants,
Your paper promises
Are the white powders,
Heated once,
Now coursing through skid row
Veins.
They are the greasy white sheets
On countless cheap hooker beds.
They are the stiff white uniforms
Of countless uncaring doctors you send
To heal uncaring patients.

> *written after George Jeffries
> of Port Simpson spoke at
> the founding meeting of the
> Union of BC Indian Chiefs,
> Fall 1969, in Kamloops*

Policy Development for Museums:
A First Nations Perspective

E. RICHARD ATLEO

"First Nations people will treat museum people and policy with respect even though respect was not reciprocated for most of the first five hundred years of contact."

DR. ATLEO of the Nuu Chah Nulth nation was born on the West Coast of Vancouver Island at Ahousat, British Columbia in 1939. The name "Atleo," translated as "Twisted Branch," refers to the rope used to tow whales captured by his ancestors who were Whaling chiefs. He spent twelve years in the Alberni Indian Residential School and graduated from the Alberni Senior Secondary School in 1959. His Bachelor of Arts, Master of Education, and Doctor of Education (the first doctorate awarded a native Indian of British Columbia) were all received from the University of British Columbia through regular programs without the aid of special support designed for native students. His thesis title was "Grade 12 Enrolments of Status Indians in British Columbia: 1949-1985." In the past he has been a teacher and principal at the elementary school level and a lecturer at the college and university level. Currently he is conducting a major native education research project in British Columbia initiated by the Native Brotherhood of British Columbia.

*   *   *

Museums that contain First Nations heritage require policy that will address issues of repatriation. Repatriation is a child of self-determination and cultural revival, both of which are contemporary, world-wide phenomena. Self-determination, which includes the right to self-identity, or the right to possess and name one's own images, is a driving force for cultural revival. Although cultural practices have been modified over time to suit changing social, political, and economic conditions, the cultural assumptions of First Nations cultures, it is argued, remains essentially the same. Cultural assumptions are not usually articulated and may be expressed as a worldview. For example, a basic assumption that the universe is essentially relational, interconnected, and holistic will generate different behaviours and attitudes toward the environment than a view which sees the universe made up of unrelated bits of reality. The former worldview encourages an attitude of respect for all life while the latter worldview may encourage an attitude toward the environment of non-respect.

These assumptions of culture are also clearly translated into social attitudes and behaviours. The relational worldview translates into an attitude which sees the smallest social unit as the extended family, whereas the other worldview translates logically into an attitude which sees the smallest social unit as the individual. Operating within the latter worldview, social scientists today have no practical method of balancing the requirements of individual freedom while meeting the requirements of the group. Yet First Nations societies practised a balance between individual and group rights long before it became a matter of general academic discussion in the old world. Thus, while the contemporary First Nations people may appear to differ little in outward behaviours from other Canadians, their internal assumptions of culture may still be fundamentally different from the prevailing assumptions of Western culture.

In addition to repatriation being a child of self-determination and cultural revival, it may also be said that repatriation is indirectly a child of a major error in judgement, in prognostication. Cole (1985) observed that the rationale for collecting First Nations artifacts during the end of the last century was the notion of a dying race, the vanishing Indian. He states:

Anthropological collecting had special impetus behind it: the realization that time was essential, that civilization was everywhere pushing the primitive to the wall, destroying the material culture and even extinguishing the native stock itself. Once the culture of these people was gone, wrote Adolf Bastian, the most gloomy of museum sages, it could not be recalled to fill gaps required by an inductive ethnological science. This sense of urgency, this notion of a scientific mission was a constant theme of nineteenth- and early twentieth-century anthropology. "In a few years it will be impossible," wrote John Wesley Powell, "to study our North American Indians in their primitive history." Stewart Culin decided that his archeology could wait; things could be left in the ground for later excavators, "but the Indian — as a savage — is soon to disappear" and "there will soon be nothing left upon the reservations." (Cole 1985, p. 287)

Rather than disappear, the "primitives and savages" began to increase in population during the first half of the twentieth century. Then during the late 1960s and early 1970s these primitives and savages rose up along with indigenous peoples all over the world and demanded freedom from their colonial masters (Barman, Hebert & McCaskill 1987). With both a growing population and a growing sense of self-determination resulting in cultural revival, the error in judgement, in prognostication about the vanishing people, helped to create museums to hold indigenous collections which, in turn, indirectly created the contemporary issue of repatriation.

In attempts to arrive at museological policy that might be acceptable to both the museum and the First Nations communities, it remains to propose a methodology. The methodology is suggested by a theory of context proposed in Atleo's 1990 doctoral dissertation at the University of British Columbia. The concept of context is not new, but its articulation into a testable theory is new. The theory of context proposes that society is an entity that directly and indirectly affects its individual parts. The corollary is that the response of the individual parts to prevailing societal conditions is important.

FIGURE 1

Dominant Society is a Context
(keeper of indigenous collections)

Society affects, and is affected by its parts

Museum is a Contextualized Part
(native collections)

Figure 1 is a simple illustration of the theory of context implying an interconnected, holistic, and relational view which reflects a First Nations perspective of reality. The dominant society refers to Canadian society as one entity, while the museum is one of its individual parts. Contained or contextualized within the museum are native collections representing First Nations heritage. The dominant society owns the concept of museology, while the First Nations people own the heritage represented in the relevant collections. There is no ambiguity about the meaning of ownership when it is defined by source and creation. The concept of museology is sourced in, and created by, the dominant society, while the concept of indigenous cultural property is sourced in, and created by, in this case, First Nations people. It is precisely the ownership of heritage and ownership of relevant collections that characterize the issue of repatriation. Under what conditions did First Nations heritage pass into collectors' hands? Were the social, political, economic, and hence psychological conditions unfairly in favour of collectors?

Repatriation demands an appropriate line of examination which will incorporate its historical roots. The theory of context is especially useful for examinations that must account for historical events in order to understand contemporary issues.

If a time line is drawn representing the period 1875 to 1990, one can depict related activities of society and its relevant parts. Figure 2 illustrates the point.

FIGURE 2

Prevailing Conditions of Society Over Time

1875..1990

Indigenous peoples considered primitive and savage.

Theory of evolution applied to indigenous peoples.

Primitives are disappearing so collections urgent!

Native declines until — *1915* — then population begins increase.

No laws to protect cultural property — Boas robs graves with impunity.

1951 Indian Act — protects
some cultural property.

1875 to roughly *1970*
the prevailing social climate towards First Nations people is exclusive. Moreover First Nations people are subjected continually to deliberate attempts at cultural genocide. First Nations people are coaxed to give up cultural property by collectors and missionaries who threaten hellfire and damnation if such property is retained.

1970 onwards — cultural
revival takes place.
Repatriation is an issue

Evidently the European did not hold First Nations people to be either equal or fully human but perceived them to be lower on an imaginary evolutionary scale. The theory of evolution is important to the issue of repatriation because it encouraged an attitude of disrespect towards First Nations people. If First Nations people were not highly valued as humans their artifacts were highly valued as scientific curiosities. Although ethnologists today deny the application of the theory of evolution to First Nations people, there has been very little scholarly work to show that precontact peoples were as human as any other human, including the European. In fact, there is reason to believe that precontact peoples and societies were much more complex than First Nations peoples and societies today. For example, precontact peoples on the coast each had to hold within their memories for ready use thousands of facts and data in several areas of human activity at the same time. It was necessary to know thousands of place names, thousands of people's names, untold thousands of biological names, untold thousands of rules and regulations about different rituals and traditions, untold numbers of stories and songs, and a great many other things. Today, the external world has increased in technological complexity, but the internal world of the First Nations person has been radically reduced. There is no need to remember thousands of place names any more because one need only buy a map or guide book. In fact, if one lacks data, one can buy it, and if one lacks skill one can buy that too. Precontact peoples did not have such options and had to acquire facts, data, and skills to maintain their cultures. What is interesting about this line of reasoning is that it runs counter to the theory of evolution as it was first proposed by Darwin. In validation of the theory of evolution, in 1904 at the St. Louis World Exposition, First Nations people, along with other indigenous people from around the world, were put on display as living examples (Cole 1985). This display of human flesh as theoretical validations was done in spite of contributions made to the Western world by this same flesh. The old world, as it was known then, was invigorated by a wealth of nutritious new foods found in the new world. Although new foods were eventually acceptable in the old world, First Nations medicines were not. It has been said that scientists today have not discovered any medicinal plant in North America that was unknown to First Nations people (Cohen 1952). Arguments like these indicate that traditional precontact First Nations societies were not only human but may have evolved from complex to simple. It is evident that First Nations societies have lost much of their ancient knowledge, the practice of which astonished some of the more discerning first European visitors.

The implication is that the so called primitives and savages were not primitives and savages, but victims of a theoretical error. If the theory of evolution has any validity (and there are sound arguments against its validity, one of which is the second law of thermodynamics and its notions of entropy), it apparently does not apply to precontact First Nations people. Indigenous peoples simply expressed their lives differently from Europeans. As the European began to dominate First Nations people socially, politically, and economically, the devaluation of indigenous peoples attributable to the theory of evolution eventually produced what has since become known as "the Indian problem." The Hawthorn Report of 1966 and 1967 provides some insight into the social, political, and economic problems encapsulated in the phrase "the Indian problem." The significance of these historical data to repatriation may be explained in the light of the theory of context.

The theory of context holds that the prevailing attitudes and practices of a dominant society toward a minority are associated with concomitant attitudes and practices of that minority. In general, therefore, when society has negative attitudes and practices toward a minority, these negative attitudes and practices may be expected to be associated with negative attitudes and practices within the minority. For example, if a dominant society considers a minority to be lazy, then it is expected that that minority will also consider itself to be lazy. This simple proposition is evidently true when the historical relationship between the Euro-Canadian and First Nations people is examined.

An obvious question at this point is to ask how cultural property might have been treated in general if indigenous peoples were properly viewed as human beings equal to Europeans instead of as primitives and savages who were not considered equal. A related question is to ask how Europeans treat each other's cultural property. It may be assumed that human beings that respect each other as human beings will also respect human cultural property.

The implication is that respect between human beings suggests guidelines for museum policy. The following section will serve as examples.

MUSEUM POLICY SUGGESTIONS

Human Remains

The Criminal Code of Canada, section 182 (b), reads as follows:

Every one who improperly or indecently interferes with or offers any indignity to a dead human body or human remains, whether buried or not, is guilty of an indictable offence and liable to imprisonment for a term not exceeding five years. R.S.,C.C-34,S.178.

The suggested museum policy is that all human remains be treated at all times with dignity and respect.

Discussion — In practice there is no ambiguity attributed to the meaning of "dignity and respect" in the Western world. Under ordinary circumstances, European human remains are accorded respectful burials without scientific research ever being raised as an issue. If scientific research and human remains are not an issue in Europe, then they should not be an issue anywhere else. It should be elementary and self-evident that scientific research was created to serve the human being and not vice versa. Scientific research has neither existence nor value by itself, for it is the human being who provides both.

Eternal and universal respect for human remains does not preclude scientific research of the same. Where scientific research of human remains is to be done, the research from inception to conclusion should be guided by the value of respect. The Criminal Code of Canada and research guidelines developed by ethics committees at institutions of higher learning may define more particularly respectful treatment of human remains.

But what of human remains that have long been held in institutions for the purpose of scientific research? The suggested policy above is still applicable. In the course of human affairs what kind of treatment is applied when one group moves from a position of disrespect to a position of respect for another group? The treatment applied to human beings and their remains would be consistent with criminal law and ethics committee guidelines.

For example, *where the direct descendants of human remains are known, the treatment of the human remains should be determined by these descendants. If the direct descendants decide that the human remains should be buried, then the remains must be buried lest a prosecution ensue under the Criminal Code.*

Scientific research at the expense of human dignity devalues the human. Devaluation of a human is destructive. The holocaust during the Second World War and the treatment of blacks in South Africa today attest clearly to the destructiveness of disrespect between human groups. First Nations people here in Canada have been devalued as human beings, and the consequences have been disastrous to First Nations families and communities. So complete has been the effects of the devaluation of First Nations people that they rank first in all the social ills, including suicide, incarceration, drug addiction, alcoholism, family dysfunctions, and failure within the educational system.

Where human remains that have long been held for research purposes in institutions have no known or traceable descendants, then the state should assume responsibility.

The state has already assumed responsibility for the treatment of the deceased in its Criminal Code, and it may be recommended that the state extend its code to include the treatment of human remains of indeterminate heritage. The rationale for so extending the Criminal Code is that the treatment of human remains reflects the treatment of human beings. Where human beings have been devalued, as were the First Nations people through such phrases as "primitive savages" and "wild barbarians," their graves could be robbed with impunity in the name of scientific research

(Cole 1985). Museum policy that "has always been concerned with the study and portrayal of human achievements from around the world" (MOA, 1982) would itself mark a human achievement by adopting guidelines which encourage respectful treatment of all human remains irrespective of time and heritage.

Cultural Property

The revised Indian Act of 1951 and the Indian Act of 1985 make some provisions for the protection of indigenous cultural property, namely,

(a) an Indian grave house,

(b) a carved grave pole,

(c) a totem pole,

(d) a carved house post, or

(e) a rock embellished with paintings or carvings.

This legislation does not apply to cultural properties "that are manufactured for sale by Indians" (Indian Act 1951). There are two observations to be made about the legislation, and each observation has implications which will be discussed.

The first observation is that legislation was seen necessary to protect the sale of certain cultural property. The second observation related to the contextual conditions of society necessitating this legislation. Atleo's (1990) thesis indicates that the prevailing social, political, and economic conditions in which First Nations people were contextualized during the time of the 1951 enactment were negative or exclusive. The meaning of exclusion refers to the condition of a dominant society, which by its power excludes a minority group from normal participation within the life of that society. At the same time as a minority is being excluded, the dominant society may also desire to acquire the cultural property of this minority in order to "research the objects and entertain the public." Under such conditions of exclusion and powerlessness it appeared necessary to legislate the protection of some cultural property. What is pertinent to current museological policy in this discussion is that there seems sound reason to believe that, in general, First Nations people may have been under unreasonable psychological, social, and economic pressure to sell cultural property that was not manufactured for sale. In this sense of the discussion about repatriation, it is not merely a legal matter but also extralegal. Although there are laws to protect contemporary consumers from unreasonable sales pressures, there are no laws (except the limited and specific legislation cited above) to protect minority groups who may have suffered unreasonable pressures over generations to sell cultural property. There is ample evidence of missionary aggression against the "evils" of indigenous cultural property between 1875 until perhaps the end of the 1960s. The influence of the missionaries was great enough to cause the Canadian Parliament to enact legislation against the potlatch, which was one cultural expression and vehicle for the use of cultural property. The legislation against the potlatch was rescinded in the revised Indian Act of 1951, but other negative societal forces against First Nations people continued until well into the 1970s (Dosman 1972, Friesen 1985, Moran 1988, Atleo 1990). The Hawthorn Report of Indian Conditions in Canada (1966, 1967) describes the prevailing negative attitudes of Canadian society toward First Nations people during this period. In addition to negative societal attitudes the First Nations people also faced a devaluation of their humanity in school curriculum. Since the first policy statements about First Nations education penned by a Jesuit missionary in 1634 until 1973, attempts at cultural genocide characterized the education of First Nations people. There seems no question that First Nations people lived under conditions of pressures and influences that could be described as unreasonable. If this is the case then the extralegal measure, in the interest of fairness that characterizes modern consumer law, museum policy must acknowledge that some of its First Nations collections were probably acquired under conditions unfair to First Nations people. Therefore the following policy is suggested.

Where cultural property was acquired under conditions of unfairness to First Nations people, and where First Nations people make a reasonable verifiable claim for repatriation, the onus of proof shall rest with the museum that the claim is conclusively invalid. Where the museum is unable to conclusively prove invalidity, the cultural property shall be repatriated under conditions which are fair according to the economic position of First Nations claimants.

Discussion — The suggested policy above is biased if viewed without historical context. The theory of context will help to explain. Figure 3 illustrates the point.

FIGURE 3

Balancing Contextual Conditions Over Time

1875-1970	*1970 onwards*
Cultural property purchased under conditions biased in favour of dominant society	Cultural property repatriated under conditions biased in favour of First Nations people

When the purchase of cultural property and its repatriation is viewed in the context of different conditions over time, the rationale for the policy suggestion becomes clearer. The policy suggestion finds its precedent in current consumer protection laws which allow consumers to return certain purchases if the consumer realizes later that the article purchased is not really wanted. In the case of First Nations cultural property the psychological, social, and economic pressures to sell have, only recently, been lessened. Pressures to sell in British Columbia, for example, have existed for two hundred years. Would it not be fair to set a statute of limitations kind of policy at two hundred years in British Columbia?

Cultural property was purchased between 1875 and 1970 under economic conditions very favourable to the dominant society. Repatriation policy should therefore reflect an inverse situation in order to balance biases perpetrated in the past. Hence it is possible that repatriation may bring current market value to a museum if the claimant is wealthy enough, or if a claimant is poor repatriation may bring its original purchase price. The policy suggestion is that repatriation take place irrespective of economic capability of the claimant.

If the above policy suggestion is accepted will it mean wholesale chaos for museums? Will museums experience an overwhelming demand for most of its indigenous collections? The theory of context predicts that such a policy will not elicit unreasonable demands from First Nations people. The fear that First Nations people will respond unreasonably to the above policy suggestion is rooted in the notions of primitivism, savagery, and barbarism. Each of these terms was initially used to describe tribal groups thought to be without laws and morals. Laws and morals were thought the exclusive prerogative of the superior European. Indigenous peoples have never been without laws and morals. Anarchy has always resulted in swift destruction. Laws and morals are the antithesis of anarchy, savagery, and barbarism. In general, it has been noted by Kluckhohn (1949), Fuchs & Havighurst (1973), Sealy (1973), DeFaveri (1984), and others that North American indigenous peoples have a different view of reality from the Western world. The difference is important. Indigenous people seem to see reality as being composed of one whole in which all is connected, interrelated, and infused with sacred life by a Creator. One powerful value that is inevitable from this view of reality is that all life forms are respected because not to respect a life form was not to respect its Creator. This view of reality is still very much a part of First Nations cultures today. Another inevitable value created from this view of reality is to see the necessity for harmony in life. As the human body made up of many organs seeks to harmonize the whole, so too does the universe made up of many parts seek to harmonize the whole. One of the laws that promote harmony is that of generosity. Explorers remarked upon the generosity of even the poorest First Nations people, and in fact the Montagnais chastised their French allies for not sharing with their French citizens in their own country but permitting their poor to starve in their civilized cities. Many other First Nations values might be remarked upon, but these two will suffice for the purpose of this discussion. These two values of respect and generosity were present upon European contact in 1492, and they are still present in First Nations communities today. The theory of context prediction is that changing social, political, and economic conditions have not been able to dislodge these values for five hundred years and they are not likely to be dislodged in the next five hundred years. First Nations people will treat museum people and policy with respect even though respect was not reciprocated for most of the first five hundred years of contact. Of course these arguments do not dispel fears based upon individual statements made by individual First Nations people who may have said "museums should give everything back." Such statements have been made and perhaps always will be made so long as museums remain to remind us of the horrors of our colonial past. Such radical statements are not without some rationale. However, First Nations values embedded firmly within their assumptions of culture preclude any radical attitudes and practices in general. In other words, exceptions to the general rule, even when uttered by a First Nations leader, are not likely to prevail. The reason is the prevalence of the value of non-interference (a natural and logical consequence of respect for all life forms) within First Nations communities which means that radical individual ideas usually has little effect (interference) upon values held by the group.

A Reasonable, Verifiable Repatriation Claim

Although the suggested policies above are biased in favour of First Nations claimants, there are some guidelines that would be reasonable to establish a verifiable repatriation claim. These may be listed as the following:

Verify that claimant A is in fact claimant A.

Verify that the cultural property being claimed is the correct one.

Verify that the cultural property being claimed belongs to the claimant with at least two witnesses other than the claimant.

Verify ability of a successful claimant to pay if payment necessary.

Since it is not unreasonable for museums to establish ownership where ownership is in dispute, the following guideline is suggested.

Where ownership of cultural property being claimed for repatriation is in dispute between alleged owners, the museum cannot act on the claim until the ownership dispute is resolved by the claimants.

Where the dispute involves allegations that the cultural property was sold illegally and where sufficient evidence of ownership, and evidence that the cultural property was likely sold illegally or inadvertently is shown by the claimant(s), then the burden of proof that it was not sold illegally should rest with the museum.

Where a repatriation claim is apparently successful for the claimant(s), a public notice of claim shall be sent to the relevant band and/or tribal council for public viewing for a period of four months(?) in order that other possible claimants for the same cultural property in dispute may have an opportunity to come forward.

In fact, as soon as a repatriation claim has a reasonable base of information, it is recommended that a public notice of claim be sent to the relevant band and/or tribal council.

Summary

Repatriation is a contemporary issue rooted in recent colonial history. Misconceptions continue to abound and hamper relationships. Much of First Nations cultural property was acquired for museums under conditions that modern consumer law prohibits. Injustices of the past which can be corrected today are worth correcting simply because it is the right thing to do. Repatriation of First Nations cultural property as outlined here is a statement of respect and an opportunity to promote a little healing in the country.

BIBLIOGRAPHY

Atleo, E. R. (1990). Grade 12 Enrolments of Status Indians in B.C. Unpublished Doctoral Thesis, Vancouver, B.C.

Barman, J., Hebert, Y. M. & McCaskill, D. (1986). "The Legacy of the past: An Overview." In Barman, J., Hebert, Y. M. & McCaskill, D. (Eds.), Indian Education in Canada: Vol. 1. The legacy, 1-21. Vancouver, B.C.: University of British Columbia Press.

———— (1987). "The challenge of Indian education: An overview." In Barman, J., Hebert, Y. M. & McCaskill, D. (Eds.), Indian Education in Canada: Vol. 2. The challenge, 1-21. Vancouver, B.C.: University of British Columbia Press.

Black Elk, Frank (1983). "Observations on Marxism and Lakota tradition." In Ward, Churchill (Ed.), Marxism and Native Americans, 137-58. Boston: Southend Press.

Cohen, F. S. (1952). Indian Heritage. Mother's reprint no. 93 taken from The American Scholar, 21, (Spring), 177-91.

Cole, Douglas (1985). Captured Heritage. Vancouver, B.C.: Douglas & McIntyre.

DeFaveri, Ivan (1984). "Contemporary ecology and traditional native thought." Canadian Journal of Native Education, 12, (1), 1-9.

Dosman, Edgar (1972). Indians: The Urban Dilemma. Toronto: McClelland and Stewart Limited.

Fisher, Robin (1977). Contact and Conflict: Indian-European Relations in British Columbia, 1774-1890. Vancouver, B.C.: University of British Columbia Press.

Frideres, James S. (1974). Canada's Indians: Contemporary Conflicts. Scarborough, Ontario: Prentice Hall.

Friesen, John W. (1985). When Cultures Clash: Case Studies in Multiculturalism. Calgary, Alberta: Detselig Enterprises Limited.

Fuchs, Estelle & Havighurst, R. J. (1973). To Live On This Earth: American Indian Education. New York: Anchor Press/Doubleday.

Government of Canada (1981a). Indian Acts and Amendments, 1868-1950. Ottawa: Indian and Northern Affairs Canada.

——— (1981b). Contemporary Indian Legislation, 1951-1978. Ottawa: Indian and Northern Affairs Canada.

——— (1983). Indian Self-Government in Canada: Report of the Special Committee. Ottawa: Indian and Northern Affairs Canada.

——— (1985). Indian Act: R.S., c. 1-6 amended by c. 10 (2nd Supp.) 1974-75-76, c. 48: 1978-79, cc. 47, 110: 1984, cc. 40, 41: 1985, c. 27: August 1985. Ministry of Supply and Services Canada, 1985.

Hardwick, F. C. (Ed.) (1973). The Helping Hand: The Debt of Alexander Mackenzie and Simon Fraser to Canadian Indians. Vancouver, B.C.: Tautalus Research Limited.

Hawthorn, H. B. (Ed.) (1966). A Survey of the Contemporary Indians of Canada. Vol. 1. Ottawa: Indian Affairs Branch.

——— (1967). A Survey of the Contemporary Indians of Canada. Vol. 2. Ottawa: Indian Affairs Branch.

Hawthorn, H. B., Belshaw, C. S., & Jamieson, S. M. (1958). The Indians of British Columbia: A Study of Contemporary Social Adjustment. Toronto: University of Toronto Press.

Kluckhohn, Clyde (1949). "The philosophy of the Navaho Indians." In Northrop, F. S. C. (Ed.). Ideological Differences and World Order, 356-84. New Haven & London: Yale University Press.

Lane, Barbara (1967). Aspects of Contemporary Indian Cultures with Emphasis on Implications for Teaching. Proceedings of Conference on the Indian Child and His Education. Extension Department of UBC.

Moran, Bridget (1988). Stoney Creek Woman: Sai'k'uz Ts'eke: The Story of Mary John. Vancouver, B.C.: Tillacum Library

Patterson, E. Palmer (1972). The Canadian Indian: A History Since 1500. Ontario: Collier-MacMillan Canada Ltd.

Sealey, D. Bruce (1973a). "The settlement of the Americas." In Sealey, D. Bruce & Kirkness, Verna J. (Eds.). Indians Without Tipis: A Resource Book by Indians and Metis, 1-6. Winnipeg: William Clare (Manitoba) Limited.

———— (1973b). "Indians of Canada: An historical sketch." In Sealey, D. Bruce & Kirkness, Verna J. (Eds.). Indians Without Tipis: A Resource Book by Indians and Metis, 9-37. Winnipeg: William Clare (Manitoba) Limited.

Warren, Karen J. (1989). "A Philosophical Perspective on the Ethics and Resolution of Cultural Properties Issues" in Messenger, Phyllis Mauch. The Ethics of Collecting Cultural Property, Albuquerque: University of New Mexico Press.

Weatherford, Jack (1988). Indian Givers: How the Indians of the Americas Transformed the World. New York: Crown Publishers, Inc.

Box Of Darkness

Doctors, curators, anthropologists,
Photographers, art historians, directors.
They've created the "renaissance";
They're the Renaissance persons.

They argue, pontificate, posit,
Hypothesize, theorize, assert, affirm,
Maintain, declare, confirm, ratify,
Present, contend, propose, indicate,
State, put forward, announce, validate,
Verify, corroborate, prove, substantiate,
Debate, avow, state, reveal, make clear,
Enlighten, inform, explain, proclaim,
Clarify, imply, deny, establish,
They claim, they take.

These are not the friends of "the Indian;"
These are The Friends of the Museum.
These are the golddiggers, gravediggers.
These are the new colonists.

They show our most treasured . . .
They reveal our sacred symbols.
They undress our spirits.
No chief has as warm a fire.

Not ours such hospitality.
Not ours to display, to pickle,
To interpret.
Or not.

Lately the rule is, "Don't interpret!"
It's all art now.
But that's an interpretation,
Not ours.

Sure, they can find a token taker,
Or two.
Brown mouths mouthing white words;
Brown faces posing for promotional shots.

"We are striking up a new relationship
With the First Nations Peoples."
"We are questioning our role in . . ."
"What we have here is the Native voice"

What you have there is
A reservation for symbols.
No dancing spirits reveal themselves
There.

Your hallowed halls are hollow.
You strive for pithy strident
Statements revealing a story,
Not yours.

You have the money;
You lack wealth.
You have the food,
And no servers to offer it.

Concrete, glass, video camera.
Visible, and invisible, Indians,
First Nations people.
In fact, you have control.
Sort of.

Voices without songs to sing;
Dancing robes and masks without dancers.
Symbols without spirits.

You live and work in our graveyard.
Picking the last remnants of flesh and blood
From my mother's bones.
This is your secret, not mine.
Don't offer me candy for silence.

Take your sweaty palm from my face;
Stand where I can see you.
Take your plastic defender's mask off.
The masquerade is stale, finished.

Let the political prisoners you hold,
Let them go.
Let me batter down your walls,
And set you free of your own
Captivity.

Crimes against the self,
Crimes against others,
Crimes against the state,
Crimes against Humanity,
Crimes against all Creation,
Which of these
Is the greatest?

Summer 1980,
at UBC's Museum of
Anthropology

Assimilation Tools: Then and Now

SHIRLEY JOSEPH

"During the era of settlement, the clear mandate of government was to assert Euro-Canadian superiority through Acts for the 'gradual enfranchisement of Indians' which would be manifest not only in a devaluation, but an elimination of Indian societies."

SHIRLEY JOSEPH, of Wet'suwet'en and Carrier ancestry, was born in 1948 and raised on the Hagwilget reserve in Northwestern British Columbia. Her interest in the effects of federal legislation upon the lives of Indian people was first sparked by Jeanette Lavall's 1970 court challenge to section 12(1)(b) of the Indian Act. From 1978 through the present she has been involved at the district, regional and national levels in pursuing changes to the Indian Act. This included extensive research, writing of submissions and briefs, conducting workshops, participating in the 1979 100-mile demonstration from Oka to Ottawa. She also worked for the Native Women's Association of Canada preparing submissions on the issue to the Standing Committee on Indian Affairs and reporting on the National Aboriginal Inquiry into the Impacts of Bill C-31 for the western regions of Canada.

Much of this article is condensed from the Inquiry findings as presented in the B.C. Regional Report.

*　*　*

Over the course of history if there is one thing that Canada's aboriginal people have learned and learned well it is that words flow easily, even eloquently. However, actions change and results are a different story.

What greater intrusion can there be than the arrogance of assuming the right to tell another people of another culture and tradition who is and who is not a member of their community and who can and can not live on their lands? (David Crombie, Intercom, Indian and Northern Affairs Canada, June 1985)

On 12 June 1985, one hundred and sixteen years of legislated discrimination against Indian women on the basis of race, sex, and marital status came to an end. At that date, Bill C-31, an Act to Amend the Indian Act, received the consent of the House of Commons.

David Crombie, then Minister of Indian and Northern Affairs, outlined the three fundamental principles of the legislation as being (1) the removal of sexual discrimination from the Indian Act; (2) the restoration of Indian status and band membership rights to eligible individuals; and (3) the recognition of band control over membership.

In reality, Bill C-31 has proven to be a modernized and more sophisticated instrument for the advancement of the age-old crusade of government to assimilate Indian people into Euro-Canadian society. Restoration of equality rights is limited both by restrictive government policies and by discriminatory provisions maintained within the Act. The concept of equality is further undermined by "class distinctions" under the membership section of the revised Indian Act. Prior to 1985, government classified Indian people as being either "status" or "non-status." Following the Act amendments, Indian people fall into one of four classifications: Status with Band Membership, Status only, Non-Status Band Members, or Non-Status Indians.

The third principle which allows bands to assume control over membership is equally flawed and ill conceived. In order to implement membership codes, bands are required to receive approval of 50 percent plus one of their membership. This extraordinary requirement is reserved for band governments alone and applies to no other legally constituted government in Canada. Although bands may confer membership, the right to determine status remains with the federal government.

Finally, based upon government's interpretation of its fiduciary responsibility, the full range of benefits and services associated with status is dependent upon reserve residency. Inadequate land base and already meagre resources of the majority of bands serve to limit the access of returning band members not only to their home bands but to the full range of benefits associated with status. Bands striving to accommodate returning members must, in many cases, contend with derision among their electorate. Returning band members are seen as competitors for already scarce and inadequate band resources.

In her thesis "Bill C-31: The Trojan Horse," Pamela Paul ascribes the manifestation of anger and frustration to:

1. a resentment towards the federal government for inadequate and unfair implementation of the bill; and

2. a resentment directed towards reinstated individuals resulting in internal conflicts at the band level. (Paul 1990:2)

As a follow-up to the above, it is the intent of this paper to present a brief synopsis of the effects of the 1985 Act amendments against an equally abbreviated profile of the historical development of the Indian Act. This summary demonstrates how injustices to Indian people are perpetuated despite the introduction of Bill C-31, which was intended to rectify historical infringement on the rights of Indian people.

Background

In 1876 all laws affecting Indian people were combined under one piece of legislation, known today as the Indian Act. The consolidated Act of 1876 addressed three areas — Land, Membership, and Local Government. Clause 6 of the 1869 Enfranchisement Act thus became section 12(1)(b) of the Indian Act.

Under the guise of "assisting Indians," the section on membership is but one example of the injustices perpetrated against Indian people by the federal government. A study of the historical development of the Indian Act reveals that the underlying intent of federal legislation was not to "assist" Indian people but rather to "eliminate" Indians. This was to be achieved through the total assimilation of Indian people into Euro-Canadian society.

During the era of settlement, the clear mandate of government was to assert Euro-Canadian superiority through Acts for the "gradual enfranchisement of Indians" which would result in not only a devaluation, but also an elimination of Indian societies. The drive towards assimilation was underscored with the desire to divest aboriginal people of the rights of ownership and jurisdiction over their territories. History shows that in the span of a twenty-five-year period, from 1869 to 1894, the government of Canada, as "trustee" of Indian people, subjugated the Indian population under legislation entitled "An Act for the Better Protection of Indian People."

First, with the introduction of section 12(1)(b) in 1869, tribes became fragmented into status and non-status or "registered" and "non-registered" Indians. While the results of this particular clause wrought havoc in all regions of the country, its effects were more pronounced in the province of British Columbia. The traditional matriarchal system of many British Columbia tribes was supplanted and replaced in legislative form with a patriarchal system.

Pursuant to section 12(1)(b) of the Indian Act, an Indian woman who married a man not recognized by government as being Indian ceased to be an Indian within the meaning of any statute or law in Canada. Upon her endorsement of the government form, "Statement of Marriage to a Non-Indian," the woman was stricken from the government's record of registered Indians. In exchange for the freedom to marry a man of her choice, the woman was required by law to forfeit her birthright. The ramifications associated with loss of status applied not only to the woman but to all children born of the marriage. By law, neither the woman nor her children were allowed to live on reserve land, and thus were not entitled to hold or inherit property on reserve. All other rights associated with status and band membership were sacrificed — the right to participate in band business, to access programs and services available to Indian people and involvement in the cultural and social affairs of the Indian community. As a final insult, the woman could not be buried on reserve land with predeceased family members. Indian men, on the other hand, under no threat of penalty, were free to choose a partner of their choice. If the woman was non-Indian, she was rewarded with status and acquired the same rights and privileges which were stripped from Indian women.

Fifteen years after the introduction of section 12(1)(b), a bill was passed banning the potlatch. For many tribes in British Columbia, the potlatch embodies the cultural, social, political, economic, legal, spiritual, ceremonial, and educational tenets of the tribes. The government of Canada recognized that tribal structures were both strong and intricate; therefore the potlatch had to be abolished to facilitate the movement of settlers into the country. Any Indian person found to be involved in a potlatch could be charged with a criminal offence and imprisoned. Parliament justified this action with claims that it was "protecting Indian people from themselves."

The 1890s heralded the beginning of the residential school era. Following the implementation of laws designed to eliminate the nucleus of tribes by banning of the potlatch, the government moved to destroy the structure and significance of family. The removal of children from their homes and villages was the single most destructive action taken by government in its drive to assimilate the Indian population into Euro-Canadian society. The move signalled the beginning of family breakdowns which in many instances took in their wake the language.

The end of World War II would signal modest change in the treatment of aboriginal people by the government of Canada. As a result of the atrocities committed during this war, the world community examined its collective conscience and in 1948 produced the United Nations Declaration of Human Rights. The government of Canada, in standing with the world community as signator to the Declaration, was forced to examine its treatment of aboriginal people. The provision banning the potlatch was subsequently removed in 1951 during the last major revision of the Indian Act. In 1960, Indian people were recognized as having the capacity to participate in the democratic process and were given the right to vote in federal elections. Indian involvement in education during the early 1970s resulted in a phasing out of residential schools. The last remaining vestige of colonialist policy, section 12(1)(b), was stricken from the Indian Act on 12

June 1985. Once again, the Indian Act amendments were not based solely in the desire of the government to alter its relationship with Indian people. The impetus for amendments to the Act stemmed both from Canada's obligations under international treaty and an internal requirement that the Indian Act be in accord with the Canadian Charter of Rights and Freedoms.

At first blush, the revised Indian Act appeared to pass the test of fairness. This revision established that:

1. No one gains or loses status through marriage;
2. Persons who previously lost status through sexual discrimination and enfranchisement are entitled to regain status;
3. First-time registration of children whose parents lost status is now possible;
4. No one will have status unless at least one parent has, or would have had, status; and
5. The concept of enfranchisement is now entirely abolished; no one can renounce or lose status. (Native Women's Association of Canada, Guide to Bill C-31, 1986:5)

While the provisions of the new Act resolved the most glaring of discriminatory clauses and conferred upon Indian bands the authority to determine their citizenship codes, it created unprecedented and new classifications of Indian people. Prior to the introduction and passage of new legislation Indian people were, for governmental purposes, divided into "Status" and "Non-status" groups. Today these two distinctions are doubled:

1. Status with band membership — Indians who have the right to both registered status and band membership;
2. Status only — Indians who have the right to be registered without the automatic right to band membership;
3. Non-status band members — Indians eligible to be registered under a band list in accordance with the Band Citizenship Code but who do not have the right to registered status; and
4. Non-status Indians — Indians who are still not entitled to be registered. The first generation cut-off clause dictates that only the first generation descendants of an individual are entitled to be registered. Second and succeeding generations will never be allowed status, nor will they be allowed to pass a right to status on to their children.

Leading up to and following passage of Bill C-31, David Crombie, then Minister of Indian Affairs, gave the assurance that "no band would be worse off" as a result of Bill C-31. Implementation of the new Act would once again underscore the degree of government ineptness in managing the affairs of Indian people. The Department of Indian and Northern Affairs grossly underestimated not only the number of individuals who would seek reinstatement but also the resources which would be required to "right the wrongs of past discrimination."

According to the government's 1985 projections, roughly 26,000 people who lost their rights as a result of sexual discrimination or enfranchisement, as well as their descendants numbering 50,000 to 60,000, would be affected by the amendments. The current figures provided by Pamela Paul in her thesis are as follows:

Between June 1985, when the Indian Act was amended, and June 30, 1990, the Indian Registration unit has received 75,761 applications representing a total of 133,134 persons seeking registration. Of these 133,134 persons, 73,554 have been approved and registered under Bill C-31 (Department of Indian and Northern Affairs, S3 Reports to June, 1990). About 62% of the registrants are female (Canadian Facts, Survey, preliminary top line results, August, 1990). (Paul 1990:7)

In compliance with section 23 of the revised Act, the minister was obligated to prepare a report on the implementation of the bill. This report was to contain:

(a) the number of people who have been registered under section 6 of the Indian Act, and the number entered on each Band List under subsection 11(1) of that Act, since April 17, 1985;
(b) the names and number of bands that have assumed control of their membership under section 10 of the Indian Act; and
(c) the impact of the amendments on the lands and resources of Indian Bands. (Indian Act 1985: ss. 22 and 23)

Although the minister was able to provide statistical information in his report, aboriginal people whose lives had been affected by the legislation were not included in the evaluation. As a consequence, a second report was to be prepared and tabled in Parliament during the fall of 1990. This evaluation would be conducted in four separate modules. The first, a National Aboriginal Inquiry on the Impacts of Bill C-31, was established jointly by the Assembly of First Nations, Native Women's Association of Canada and Native Council of Canada. The second module of this evaluation was a survey of registrants; the third, a survey of selected bands and communities; and the fourth, an internal government evaluation of programs. The collection of reports from each of the modules is intended to represent an assessment of the impacts of Bill C-31 upon individuals and Indian communities throughout the four year period from 1985 to 1989.

The National Aboriginal Inquiry conducted forty-five days of community hearings in nineteen centres throughout Canada during late 1989 and early 1990. Approximately one-third of all evidence entered into the Inquiry record during the course of the western hearings was from British Columbia. The province also ranked highest in the number of submissions received in a region from both eastern and western Canada combined. Submissions ranged from the examination of the legislative impacts upon villages, to the administration of programs and services, to the effects upon personal and family life. Presenters shared their views on the effects of the previous incarnations of the Indian Act, the impact of current legislation and possible future consequences. In their assessment of the innumerable shortfalls of Bill C-31, many underscored their presentations with the fact that tribal laws take precedence over the Indian Act. The potlatch, though banned by government decree in the late 1800s, remains both intact and inviolate.

Nuu Chah Nulth culture and laws find expression through the potlatch. At a Nuu Chah Nulth potlatch it would be common to see elders and other members of the Nuu Chah Nulth communities acknowledge either verbally or otherwise the roots that they have in our various communities. We have an expression in our language, "multh-muumpts" which refers to a person's roots. We continue to practise that recognition, that law and that tradition today. . . . We believe it is incumbent upon the federal government to recognize that Nuu Chah Nulth people have a long history of laws and culture dealing with membership and association with other tribes.
(Hugh Braker, Nuu Chah Nulth Tribal Council, B.C. Regional Report 1990:7)

In no other western region were the words "genocide," "assimilation" and "racism" used more frequently in the appraisal of Bill C-31 than in British Columbia. It is a commonly held view that Bill C-31 policies and regulations serve no other purpose than to further advance the government's crusade to assimilate aboriginal people into Euro-Canadian Society. Analogies were drawn to describe the impact of Bill C-31 upon the lives of families, villages, and tribes.

As we recall somewhere in our history books about Greece, where the Trojan Horse was a gift. Bill C-31 appears to be a gift, a gift in the manner where discriminatory clauses have been removed, especially clauses that affected our Native women . . . so, Bill C-31, being a Trojan Horse, comes in as a gift . . . When we accept Bill C-31 and open it up as the Trojan Horse, instead of warriors coming out, assimilation will be coming out. With that our culture and language will be forever lost, thus we, as Native people.

(Ray Jones, B.C. Regional Report 1990:8)

Throughout the B.C. hearings, the most contentious issues arising from Bill C-31 in the view of individuals and bands were:

- Status & Band Membership: Documentation requirements; Second generation cut-off; Band Membership and Codes; Reinstatement Process; Legislative Omissions; Internal Discrimination; and, Human Rights Implications.

- Band Land and Resources

- Benefits Associated with Status and Band Membership: Access to Services and Benefits; Housing; Education; and Medical.

- Social and Cultural Impacts

The remaining section of this article provides but a glimpse into the Inquiry findings. The limitations imposed by a journal article preclude full examination of each of the multiplicity of issues and the many convolutions brought to light during the course of the Inquiry. This discourse merely scrapes the surface with its focus on status and band membership issues (documentation requirements, second-generation cut-off and band membership codes) and band land and resources.

Documentation Requirements

In order to be eligible for reinstatement, applicants were required to provide incontrovertible proof of their relationship to a family member who suffered loss of status. For many this dictated a full-scale genealogical search for records of attestation of eligibility as far back as the mid-1800s. At that time, record keeping was incomplete and inconsistent with names being recorded improperly, if at all.

Probably the most heart-rending evidence respecting documentation was that of Robert and Jane Cromarty. Before submitting their application for reinstatement they attended a workshop on conducting genealogical research, then set out to satisfy departmental criteria for documentation. Their personal resources were limited to a pension income which they had used to travel in search of documents to substantiate their request for reinstatement.

We have gone many places and I might pass on to you some of the places where we went. We went to the band offices, we searched the cemeteries. We went through the newspaper articles. We went to the provincial archives. We went to Coqualeetza. We went to the genealogy society in Vancouver.

(Jane Cromarty, B.C. Regional Report, 1990:14)

. Information acquired by the Cromartys was considered insufficient; therefore their request for reinstatement was denied. An appeal on this decision was presented one year ago along with additional documentation. In early December 1990, the Cromartys were advised by the Department of Indian Affairs and Northern Development (DIAND) that their appeal was still being processed.

For many individuals, the search for documentation began and ended with church records. The parish priest was the prime record-keeper, and many of the early wooden churches have long since burned down.

The only type of documentation kept in those days was with the Oblate priest. The Oblate priests had fairly intricate background information, but there was a fire in a church back in those days and the church burned down and a lot of the information was lost . . . So that was the only documentation that they had in terms of birth certificates and what have you. That's the problem we're having now. It is identifying my grandfather's status.

(Leo Hiebert, B.C. Regional Report, 1990:14)

The onus of proof of eligibility rests with the individual applicant. Many individuals point out that while the Department of Indian Affairs and Northern Development possesses much of the necessary information in its files, it is reluctant to provide even basic assistance to applicants. DIAND does not cross-reference applications from members of the same extended family. Therefore, each applicant is required to provide the full range of information in spite of the fact that the documents are already on file. Furthermore, each applicant must secure the information and resubmit it to the department from which it came. (Paul, 1990:47)

Second Generation Cut-Off

If Bill C-31 is the Trojan Horse for assimilation, section 6(2) is the weaponry carried by its warriors. Under section 6 of the amended Indian Act, if a person has only one parent entitled to reinstatement, he or she is classified under section 6(2) and can only transmit status to succeeding generations if his or her spouse/partner is a status Indian.

It says we'll recognize you as long as you're a half breed, but if you go below that you won't be entitled to status. That's what Section 6(2) does. The result is going to be in the future an incredible amount of inequality and the Act is designed, in my opinion, to do away with Indians.

(Hugh Braker, Nuu Chah Nulth Tribal Council, B.C. Regional Report, 1990:21)

Participants in the Inquiry admonished the government for the incorporation of the second generation cut-off clause under Bill C-31. Reactions to section 6(2) ranged from incredulity to alarm and outright hostility. In fact, it is this article that generates the accusations of genocide, assimilation, and racism.

The sexual discrimination that was to be redressed through Bill C-31 continues to be felt. There remains unequal treatment of male and female siblings. Women who lost status through marriage cannot pass status through successive generations the same way their brothers who married non-Indian women prior to 1985 can. The brothers and their non-Indian spouses and children are automatically considered band members, while the sisters' children can only acquire status. The children of the female line have conditional entitlement to band membership.

Equally deleterious is the treatment of children born out of wedlock. Policy requires not only that an unmarried woman must disclose the natural father's name but also that the father must acknowledge paternity in writing. Otherwise, the father is presumed to be white and the children are subsequently registered as section 6(2) applicants.

It must be noted that such invasion and total disregard for human dignity as demonstrated by this policy would never be tolerated in Canadian Society, yet aboriginal women are subjected to it each and every time they apply to register a child born out of wedlock. (Paul, 1990:52)

It is noted earlier that 71,508 individuals have been registered since passage of Bill C-31. Of this number 60.2 percent or 43,076 have had their status restored under section 6(2) of the Act.

Those individuals registered under Section 6(2) must marry an Indian person either a 6(1) or 6(2) to transmit their status. Aboriginal people have stated that through Section 6(2), as was the case with Section 12(1)(b) of the previous Act, their grandchildren are being given a message, marry endogamously or suffer the consequences. (Ibid:58)

In light of the implications of the second-generation cut-off rule, the path created by Bill C-31 is seen as a dead end both for individuals affected and, ultimately, for the tribe.

Last, but not least, the amendment does not only discriminate against Native females, it is even worse. The amendment right does not give back the rights to some individuals. It does not give them back their identity. As a matter of fact, in many cases they have taken away the freedom of choice for many of these people. I guess that is even worse than discrimination. In my own words this is genocide. When you have taken away everything from an individual

and you won't even let them call themselves an Indian you might as well call it genocide because that is what it is.
(Andrew Joseph, Tl'Azt'en First Nation, B.C. Report, 1990:24)

Band Membership and Codes

While Bill C-31 stipulates the manner through which bands may assume control of membership, the determination of ancestry within First Nations is carried out according to internal laws. The imposition of federal statute and its artificial distinctions is considered an unnecessary encumbrance designed only to promote division within First Nations. Presenters criticized the government for continuing its practice of flagrant disregard for the laws of First Nations.

The Nuu Chah Nulth people reject classification of our people as either 6(1) or 6(2); we reject the classification of our people as on reserve or off reserve. We reject the classification of our people as half breed, quarter breed or full breed. We reject the classification of our people as non-status or full status; we reject the classification of our people by anything other than their roots. We believe it is incumbent upon the federal government to recognize that Nuu Chah Nulth people have a long history of laws and culture dealing with membership and association with tribes. It is that system of roots or blood ties which we wish to give effect to.
(Hugh Braker, Nuu Chah Nulth Tribal Council, B.C. Regional Report, 1990:26)

In contrast, government heralded the option which would allow bands the right to develop membership codes as the first step towards self-government in that it provided the mechanism through which bands and tribes would determine their citizenship. However, the freedom to develop membership codes is circumvented not only by legislation but also by the dictates of federal policy.

Aboriginal groups contend that in granting band control of membership, the federal government failed to emphasize the fact that band councils could only take control of their membership codes within the criteria dictated to them under the Indian Act. That is, band councils would only add onto their band lists those categories of persons entitled to band membership as dictated in section 11 of the revised Act. This meant that the band councils could admit 6(1)'s a, b, c, d, e, or f and 6(2)'s and still receive funding for these individuals. However, if the bands decided to go further and admit persons who did not fit these categories then DIAND would not grant the funds necessary to the bands to provide services to those people. . . . Therefore, the only areas feasible to band councils wishing to recognize their so-called right of control of their membership was to deny rights to Native peoples under their membership codes. . . . (Paul, 1990:62)

Band Land and Resources

Without question, bands are in a worse position now than they were prior to the enactment of Bill C-31. The effect of Bill C-31 reverberates throughout the entire native community and is felt by every person who is connected to that community. Land base is an issue. Housing stock is an issue. Financial and program resources considered inadequate prior to Bill C-31 have become strained beyond reason.

Former Minister David Crombie's promise that "No Band would suffer as a result of Bill C-31" definitely does not apply in our case. Our community has suffered needlessly we might add, and we would like the suffering to stop. Our band is bursting at the seams in need of housing, land, capital, infrastructure, employment, economic development, health services, band support, recreation etc. etc. Bill C-31 can be a positive experience all around but in order for that to happen we have to be more involved with the process. Our concerns have to be taken seriously and our needs have to be met.

(Dave Pop, Soda Creek Band, B.C. Regional Report, 1990:41)

The infamous phrase of David Crombie was echoed in presentations of bands and tribal councils. Presenters called the government to task for its unfulfilled commitments. In the absence of adequate resources, bands are left to contend not only with the impatience of returning members who wish to access benefits that had been denied but also with the ire of band members who perceive that they are now being denied benefits as a result of Bill C-31.

The Fort George Band at first welcomed the advent of Bill C-31 because it meant those of our people who had been displaced both physically and psychologically, could now return to their homeland. They could, after years of being ostracized by government, bureaucrats, the non-Natives and even their own people, finally come home. What we have to ask at this time is, what have they come home to?

(Helen Seymour, Fort George Band, B.C. Regional Report, 1990:41)

In the province of B.C. there are 196 bands situated in the most geographically diverse region in Canada. In general, the reserve land base is small. The influx of people in a short period of time has placed direct pressure on the existing land base.

Although many Bands have substantial increases in population with Bill C-31 returnees, they have been expected to squeeze them onto Band land that is already crowded. Bands such as Tzeachten have approximately 98% of their land in Certificates of Possession so that there is no available land for Bill C-31 houses. Matsqui's land has such poor drainage that it is unsuitable for houses. Further there is a lack of capital dollars to service lots. . . .

(Leona Charleyboy, Sto:Lo Nation, B.C. Regional Report 1990:46)

The Carrier-Sekani Tribal Council reported that 75 percent of their twelve member bands do not have serviced building lots available and 83 percent of the inhabited villages lack adequate fire protection. Among the twelve bands there is a total of seventy-two building lots available. The total number of applicants (to 1989 December) from the tribal council area was 1,431, of which 724 have been registered.

The housing dilemma confronting band administrations in British Columbia is no less in magnitude than that articulated to the Inquiry in other regions. The degree of frustration experienced not only by band administrations but also by individuals and their families who are without adequate accommodation is enormous. It must be appreciated that Bill C-31 did not bring about the housing crisis on reserve. Inadequate housing stock and waiting lists had long been a reality and were only made worse by an increase in population. The situation the Stellaquo band finds itself in is analogous to that of many small bands.

We get two houses per year, and so we have 62 on our backlog on the reserve. It would take us 31 years to accomplish what we need. So it will be the year 2020 before we have no problems in housing. . . .
(Zaa Louie, Stellaquo Band, B.C. Regional Report 1990:56)

Benefits Associated with Status and Band Membership

Under the Indian Act, rights are determined according to residency. Policy of the Department of Indian Affairs states that fiduciary responsibility is only to those who are status band members residing on reserve.

Having Aboriginal Rights determined by residency is a direct violation of the so-called "mobility" clause of Section 6 of the Charter of Rights and Freedoms. The Government's fiduciary responsibility extends to all Aboriginal people defined as Indians, Inuit, and Metis in Section 35 of the Constitution Act, 1982, irrespective of where they live.
(Ron George, B.C. Regional Report, 1990:50)

Status Indian people residing off-reserve are only entitled to access post-secondary educational assistance and medical benefits. In British Columbia, as in other regions, the off-reserve population is significant.

According to a study we did this summer from the Department of Indian Affairs statistics and Statistics Canada, it shows that 77% of the status Indian population live off-reserve. In a majority of cases, it's a direct result of lack of services, housing and land available from already over-extended and under-funded bands.
(Ron George, United Native Nations, B.C. Regional Report, 1990:50)

Individuals who had been reinstated expected to regain the rights to which they are entitled. However, when living off reserve, they quickly find that those rights are both more difficult to exercise and restricted. Rights to housing are inaccessible. Too many reserves have small land bases and cannot accommodate those who would like to return. Problems are compounded in that many reinstatees are unaware of the requirements for program entrance; there are few information sources to assist them; and, when they do qualify, they all too often find themselves low on the list. Generally, if you live off reserve, you are ineligible to vote in band elections. There is no one to represent you.

Because of the lack of sufficient resources, the bands are extremely limited in what they can deliver. The flaws which were tolerated in existing programs, with the additional pressures of numbers, have become unbearable.

Conclusion

Problems attributable to Bill C-31 extend far beyond the parameters of policy, programs, and administrative tangles. Prior to the passage of Bill C-31, very few Indian communities had the capacity to guarantee to their constituents a standard of living considered acceptable in Canada.

For many people, Bill C-31 is a symbol both of legislation and policies which are contrary to the most basic rights and freedoms. The government, they say, has failed to consider traditional governing structures and practices, failed to recognize its responsibilities to those who live anywhere other than on reserve land, and failed even to protect the rights of individuals on reserve.

In her thesis, Paul (1990:103) concludes that the implementation of Bill C-31 has resulted in transformations of the structures of aboriginal societies ranging from minimum to maximum disruptions based on numbers of persons reinstated to quality and quantity of resources available. The social effect of Bill C-31 can, in her view, be summarized as follows:

1. Bill C-31 has disrupted community life through social and economic factors;
2. Bill C-31 has created competition for scarce resources, leading to an alienation and hostility towards reinstated individuals;
3. Bill C-31 has created a new class of aboriginal people;
4. There is ongoing residual discrimination contained within the Indian Act, which can be viewed as an assimilative tool used by the federal government. (Ibid: 104)

Most obvious is the fact that an exacting sacrifice has been made and continues to be made by aboriginal people for the purpose of allowing Euro-Canadian governments to advance their plans for the ongoing development of Canada. The path to resolution of the outstanding grievances of aboriginal people is strewn with obstacles, some of which have, like huge immovable boulders, been there since the first European contact. As time passed, new walls were built to divide and weaken the strength and energies of aboriginal people.

To correct the injustices suffered by native people, it is essential that the impassable boulder of a paternalistic government attitude which presumes to define who aboriginal people and their families are be demolished. It is also essential that the walls created by rules and definitions be torn down in order to remove some of the complications and frustrations experienced by native people as they move forward as the First Nations of Canada — for move forward the aboriginal people will continue to do. As history shows, in spite of the years of systematic effort to eliminate Indians, Canada's aboriginal people continue to persevere, to adapt, and to survive.

BIBLIOGRAPHY

Department of Indian and Northern Affairs Canada (1985). Intercom, Canadian Government Publishing Centre, Ottawa.

Government of Canada (1989). Indian Act.

Joseph, Shirley (1990). British Columbia Regional Report on the impact of Bill C-31, unpublished, Ottawa. Prepared for the Native Women's Association of Canada (NWAC), the Assembly of First Nations (AFN), and the Native Council of Canada (NCC).

Paul, Pamela (1990). Bill C-31: The Trojan Horse: an Analysis of the Social, Economic and Political Reaction of First Nations People as a Result of Bill C-31. A thesis submitted in partial fulfilment of the requirements for the Degree of Master of Arts in the Department of Anthropology, The University of New Brunswick.

A Part Apart

I grew up near Canada
Close to Port Alberni
On Vancouver Island
Close to British Columbia

We saw a lot of Canadians
Over time. Nearly every day
A Canadian interrupted our lives
Walking by but looking in

And some times they brought papers
Or just sent them in the mail
We had a radio too
And then a T.V.

I came to the age of majority
Without the right to vote
Or cry in your beer, but
I grew up near Canada
A part apart and not of the whole

Summer 1983,
at T'üpis

Sechelt Women and Self-Government

THERESA M. JEFFRIES

"The people of Sechelt upheld the belief that the right and privilege of determining our destiny must remain within our community."

Sxixixay, a mother and grandmother whose English name is Theresa Jeffries, is a member of the Sechelt band council. She holds the distinction of being the first member of her band to graduate from high school. Born in Sechelt, she returned in 1987 after an absence of thirty-six years. She spent twenty years in Prince Rupert, where one of her many jobs was for the Department of Indian Affairs as a cultural consultant. In her sixteen years in the Vancouver area she worked with a number of native organizations and was an active volunteer seeking solutions to social and political issues affecting aboriginal people. Throughout that time she was well known for her own struggle to legally regain her birthright as an Indian.

For the past three years, Theresa has worked as an employment counsellor in Sechelt and actively participates in the Sechelt people's struggle to control and direct their own destinies.

* * *

In October 1986, my band, the Sechelt Indian band, became the only legislated self-governing band in the province of British Columbia when federal legislation was passed restoring ownership and government of Sechelt reserve lands to the Sechelt people. In 1987, the province passed the complementary Sechelt Indian Government District Enabling Act to extend municipal benefits and provincial home-owner grants to the new Indian district — it should be noted, however, that the powers exercised by the Sechelt Indian Government District flow from the band and not from the province — and subsequently enabled Sechelt lands to be registered within the provincial land title system.

I have written this article to explain to you what this means to the Sechelt people and more specifically to Sechelt women. My name is Sxixixay. I am from the village of Sechelt, Eagle clan, and daughter of the late Sara Jeffries. Through my grandmother we go back as far as there is oral history. I want to take you on a journey. This journey will encompass our past, where we are today, and our hopes and aspirations for tomorrow.

Past

The concept of self-government is not new to the Sechelt. As a people we have been self-governing since the beginning of time. My ancestors were totally self-sufficient, utilizing the resources of the environment to keep the people gainfully employed in contributing to the maintenance of our community. We gathered and harvested our sustenance from the sea and the forest; we built our communal homes from the materials around us. There were teachers, political and spiritual leaders, healers, care-givers, and entertainers all within our community and all having been trained from birth in their roles and responsibilities.

The people of Sechelt were governed from within through a system of laws which was handed down from generation to generation. Decisions were made and witnessed by hereditary chiefs in the feast hall. While the chiefs were male, it was the responsibility of the women to raise, groom, and prepare the future chiefs. Women were thus the keepers of the culture and the teachers of the culture and influenced all that transpired in the Sechelt world.

Memories of my grandmother, Mollyann, and my great-grandmother, Tah, come to mind. My grandmother was born and raised in the village of Tsonai. She was married at fifteen and had fifteen children. It was the custom at that time for a man to have more than one wife.

The missionaries' zeal to Christianize forced my grandfather, Pah, to make a serious decision. He had to choose one wife. Fortunately for me, it was my grandmother. My grandmother and grandfather were extra-ordinary people in their own right. My grandfather was an orator and interpreter. He spoke for people on issues of importance in the feast hall, and acted as a translator from Sechelt into English. They were both a strong force in my life. My grandfather insisted that I complete my education. In those days it was almost unheard of for an Indian person to go beyond grade 8, but because of his support I was the first graduate of the Sechelt band.

My grandmother loved life. In addition to her own fifteen children she raised ten of her granddaughters. She was the first woman to work off reserve, but I remember her best in a more traditional role. She was a basket weaver *par excellence* and used to trade baskets to clothe us. In the spring, when it was time, we would gather the roots. We always looked forward to it because it was an occasion for teaching and an occasion for affirmation of the family and our traditions. She would teach us to recognize the right cedar trees, pinpoint the straight roots, and gather far enough from the tree so that the tree would survive. Through stories and myths, she would teach us about our family, our history, and our responsibilities. It was always in the language of the Sechelt, and there was always a lesson to be learned.

Present

The threads which bind us to our past — our language, laws, culture, and traditions — have over time become tenuous. This is the result of government intervention and the breakdown of the family unit through residential schools. At five or six years of age children were taken from their families to be educated in church-run residential schools. In these schools, children were punished for speaking in their own language. Everything we respected was ridiculed. We were made to feel strangers in our own land. When we went home, often after eight years in that system, some of us couldn't talk to our parents. With the erosion of the language, culture, traditions, and self-esteem, we became dependent upon another government and systems which were meaningless to us. We were forced into compliance by legislation, specifically the Indian Act, and by its administrative arm, the Department of Indian Affairs.

The feast halls, laws, and system of hereditary chiefs were supplanted by duly elected chiefs and councillors. A patriarchal system was superimposed upon the matrilineal society of the Sechelt. Divisions were created within families and the community by government assuming the right to decree who would be recognized as being Indian. Parallel to this was the requirement that certain benefits or rights could only be granted after one had denied his or her ancestry. Acquisition of the right to vote, enter public drinking places, and pursue an education could only occur after an individual had been stricken from the government's list of registered Indians.

The government's treatment of women under the Indian Act was particularly devastating and tantamount to cultural genocide, because women were responsible for maintaining culture. If a woman chose to marry a non-Indian man, she was removed from government's list of registered Indians. Bear in mind that the definition of non-Indian included Indian men who had, at the hands of government, suffered loss of status. Upon marriage, the woman could no longer live in the community in which she was born, nor could she participate in any matters respecting the community. The final insult was upon death: neither she nor any of her children could be buried in a family plot on band land.

These actions of government served to create divisions not only in the community but within and between families. The responsibility of women as guardians of the culture was, in essence, negated from the perspective of government.

In similar fashion, the government bequeathed Indian status upon women who married status Indian men. Even if the woman was Euro-Canadian by birth, she became recognized as Indian and became entitled to enjoy all rights, benefits, and privileges associated with Indian status.

I speak of this from personal experience. In 1963, I married an Indian man whose mother had lost her status upon marriage. I can recall the shock and disbelief I felt upon receipt of a "blue card" from government which stated that I was no longer "deemed to be Indian." Not able to accept that anyone should have the authority to alter my birthright, I became involved in a twenty-two-year quest for justice. In 1985 the Indian Act was revised, and although changes were partially retroactive, the Act continues to detrimentally affect the lives of many people.

Given all that has transpired, you will agree that there was ground and cause to accept the situation as futile and to suppose that the stereotypical images held of us as Indian people would endure. I will not deny that the life course of some people has been negatively altered by this sense of futility. Fortunately, the majority have accepted the past as gone and have become committed to meeting the challenges associated with removing the shackles placed on us by the federal government.

The people of Sechelt uphold the belief that the right and privilege of determining our destiny must rest within our community. Rather than making our community fit federal legislation, we have made the legislation fit our community. On June 24, 1988, a ceremony commemorating the achievement of self-government was hosted by the people of Sechelt.

What does self-government mean? Self-government emerges from Indian people. Our leaders can but express it and refine it by negotiation. Always, they must go back to whence it came, back to the people for approval or rejection. The Sechelt Band Act creates the band as a legal entity having the capacity, rights, powers, and privileges of a natural person. The provisions of this Act include the right to enter into contracts or agreements, to acquire and hold property or sell it, to expend or invest money, and to borrow money. All such powers and duties are carried out in accordance with the Sechelt band constitution. The concept of the band constitution allows us as the people of Sechelt to implement change at a pace chosen by us. It respects our autonomy as a people and enables us to be economically independent. Given that the constitution alone is fifty pages in length, I will only provide a thumbnail sketch of that which is encompassed.

In accordance with this new agreement, the Sechelt band has achieved a high degree of political and administrative autonomy. Decisions can be made without having to await a yea or nay from Ottawa. The ability to establish a membership code means that we can define ourselves in tribal terms, while the ability to control the disposition of Sechelt lands means that the land and resource base which form the foundation of the band economy are under our control. Possessing a rich land and resource base, the band is engaged in land development, specialty forest products manufacturing, gravel extraction, forestry, aquaculture, aircraft leasing, and operating a charter and scheduled airline.

Although encumbrances have been removed, the Sechelt band is very concerned that powers be exercised responsibly, particularly as they relate to non-Indians. Residents on band land who are not Sechelt participate and express their interests and concerns by way of an advisory council. The council does not have legislative powers. It is strictly an advisory body to the District Council.

The band, wishing to remain an integral part of the larger Sunshine Coast social, economic, and political culture, asked that the Sechelt Indian Government District become a full member of the Sunshine Coast Regional District. Through the District, the band takes its place at the regional table, participates in the politics and government of the region, and avails itself of the services of the Regional District.

You may be wondering to what extent the practice of self-government today parallels the traditional form of government of our ancestors. The likenesses are few, since what we have today is in essence an interpretation negotiated with the federal and provincial governments which takes into account today's realities. We are administered now by an elected council rather than by our families and clans under the laws of the feast hall. The language of government is English and not Sechelt. Our meetings are conducted more in accordance with parliamentary rules than traditional law. Our education is for the most part from the public system and not from the laps of our grandmothers. In order to feed and clothe our families, we rely on outside jobs rather than on the natural resources of the land. We recognize that sacrifices have been made. We recognize as well that what was fitting for Sechelt people one hundred years ago is not, in some instances, fitting to Sechelt people today. *What has not changed and cannot be altered is our distinct cultural identity.*

The role and responsibility of women as keepers of the culture remains in place. I discussed earlier the manner in which our language has been weakened. Now, largely through the efforts of women, our language is being revived. It is said that once a language dies, so does the culture. We as a people have taken steps to strengthen the ties with our ancestors by strengthening our language and culture.

What I hope for my granddaughters is no different from what you wish for yours. It is my wish that together they will reap the benefits of our struggles. I hope they will learn to respect the differences found in ancestry, language, and traditions and will carry on working to advance common goals and aspirations for the benefit of all people.

The process of change that we, the Sechelt nation, have undertaken will not be an easy job for anyone. As a people, we must accept the difficulties that come with this process, including frustration, setbacks, and long periods of seemingly no progress. This process applies not only to the Sechelt but also to the people living on the outside communities. The erosion of the Sechelt lifestyle took decades, and it will take much time to rebuild a strong and dynamic community. The women will contribute much to the process by maintaining the traditions and continuing to train our sons and daughters to be worthy leaders.

We will remember the past so that mistakes are not repeated and all the best and strongest traditions are maintained. We will live fully in the present, seizing opportunities and growing stronger daily. We will look forward to tomorrow and to living a good life. At all times we will be thankful for the life and gifts that our Creator has given us.

It is an exciting time to be an aboriginal person, making so many seemingly impossible dreams come true. It is not too late to start implementing our visions. The best time to begin this journey is right now.

Our Story Not History

We are walking up the road
That leads to history.
Some are being led peacefully
Others are driven from within.

Some are dragged kicking and screaming.
Pulled forcefully
Down the road that leads
Away from their history.

A very few are changing history.
Redefining the meaning of history.
Making history responsible
To those caught in its sticky web.

Sadly some are prisoners of history,
Their very lives defined,
And their futures determined,
By a history compiled by their enemies.

Some are being made by history
Some are "making" history.

*circa 1968-75,
in Victoria*

Life and Death and Life

Pen on Paper, by Ki-ke-in

I Invite Honest Criticism: An Introduction

RON HAMILTON

Long ago, when Kuu-as (humankind) and all other animals knew and understood each other, Kwatyaat (the primeval West Coast superhero) engraved designs representing sea and land creatures, real and imagined, over the full expanse of a large flat rock wall on the lakeshore not far above Emin.[1] These markings on the rock were a message from him to the Huupachesath people, the traditional owners of the territory, to be respectful of all creation.

When I was a boy, in the 1950s, my mother's auntie, Ayaat, visited us annually and regaled our family with stories about these animals that thought and felt the way we do. She would become in turn Ke-in, Tlehmaamit, Ii-ishsuu-ilth, Kwiikwistupsup (Miss Crow, Mr. Red Shafted Flicker, Pitchwoman, Transformer), or any of a great number of other characters. She never portrayed them, acted like them, or copied the way they spoke — she became them! Each year, in the fall, when the commercial berry-picking season in Washington state was finished, and just in time for the annual dog salmon run up the Somass River, Ayaat would come, bringing much joy into our home. She was pure poetry.

All through my life I've been aware of the great efforts of my uncle, George Clutesi, to overcome the racism and ignorance so characteristic of Canadian treatment of us, the First Peoples of this part of the world. On behalf of all the native people in this country, he carried on a long and frustrating harangue, utilizing traditional songs and dances, painting, public speaking, acting, prose writing, and poetry. Like Kwatyaat, he wanted to send a message to future generations. Like Ayaat, he used poetry to send that message.

In 1973, after eight years of travel over much of the world (brought on by a failed career as a grade 8 student), I moved back to Aswinis, where I was born and raised. During one of our first conversations, after my

[1] Emin is the name of a whirlpool on the Sproat River. My brother Kwitchiinim lives there with his son. The large rock face is on the shoreline of Sproat Lake, close to where it spills into Sproat River.

return home, Uncle Georgie said to me, "Don't write your autobiography yet, Nephew. You're not ready yet, but your day will come." His confidence in my abilities and his always present encouragement have had much to do with my poetry.

For years I've kept a daily journal, recording important events in my family's current history and momentous occurrences in my community. I've tried to make the information in my journals available to others as much as possible. However, the poetry I've been writing since the 1960s is another story. I've almost always kept my poetry absolutely private, but recent events in the literary world and in the world of politics have convinced me that the time is right to try them out on the greater public as well as in my own community.

There is an ever-growing number of anthologies of writing by First Nations authors, as well as works by individual native writers, being published these days, and they are receiving considerable attention from literary circles and the wider public — this is encouraging. So are the events of last summer. The Mohawk people's struggle for recognition of their rights, and the ensuing fiasco that resulted from the Canadian army's attempt to quash that struggle, have brought renewed attention to native issues. That interest has spilled over into the literary world, and this too is encouraging.

Last summer, I lived with my Auntie Lizzy, my mother's elder sister. It was on her television that I watched the standoff at Oka develop. Auntie Lizzy told me she'd been trying to write stories and had soon found herself too tired to continue, "You know, Ronny, you should write the stories down for me. You could make a book, couldn't you?" She was concerned that both a local amateur historian and the renowned anthropologist, Edward Sapir, had failed to get the story straight when writing about events in our family's history. Her desire to see our stories in written form has inspired me. More immediately, it was Doreen Jensen's invitation to submit my writing for publication in the present volume that is responsible for it now being before the public.

Now, it is important for me to state clearly that my writing is mostly informed by my experience as a member of my family — a very large though tightly knit extended family. It is also shaped by my communities, in descending order of importance: my tribe, the Nuuchahnulth-speaking community, all Northwest Coast native people, all oppressed people anywhere in the world. I am aware too that I am a citizen of the world community, and I feel a sense of responsibility to this our largest community. I mean to exclude no one from enjoying my poems; I hope they offer insights for all who wish to better understand the cultural and political aspirations of First Nations peoples.

The one concern I have about the publication of my poetry is motivated by our political history. For a very long time now, we have pressed the case for recognition of our aboriginal rights — including sea and land claims. Successive governments have failed to listen to our arguments, partly because — we are repeatedly reminded — we do not know how to state our case according to the rules. Just as Canadian courts have had to adopt some new terms and procedures in order to expedite land claims cases, I believe the Western literary traditions will have to adopt some new forms of writing, not necessarily recognizable as prose or poetry, in order to speed up the approaching understanding so much looked forward to by natives and non-natives alike. I don't want to have to launder my thoughts and bleach my words "white" in order to have them published. The flip side of that coin is that I don't want my writing published merely because I'm a native Indian. I don't want to be a token Indian writer. I don't want to be patronized. I invite honest criticism, and look forward to improving and learning from it.

Chuu,
Ki-ke-in
(Ron Hamilton)
at Musqueam,
Winter 1991

Opetchesaht Tribe Ii-ishsuu-ilth design, by Hapkwachuu

Lino block print inspired by an early Henry Speck work.

Return To The River

My sister comes home every year,
When the sockeye return in numbers,
To swell our river with their numbers,
And she goes down to our river.

My sister returns to our river each year,
When it's time to fish for sockeye,
With dip net, gill net, or drag seine,
And she goes out in our waters.

My sister wades out in our cold rushing river,
When the seine is set around the jumpers,
Swimming home to share their wealth,
And she stoops to help pull in the net.

My sister strains with her back bent taut,
When our island is hidden by splashing,
Visitors arrayed in silver ribbons,
And she comes home every year.

> *Summer 1978,*
> *at Aswinis, for my sister*
> *Sandra*

Bumble Bee

Alvin you fly from room to room
Humming and giggling, gurgling, laughing
"I'm Bumble Bee, hay Dad?"
Zoom, you're gone again

> *Spring 1986,*
> *at Aswinis, for my son*
> *Alvin Alfred*

A Piece Of My Heart

At half a century in age
Kwitchiinim called us together
In this house
To say, "I'm sorry, for all
The hurtful things I've done
And said through all these years."

With white hair glowing proudly
My brother stands before us
With his son
To give thanks to the family
For standing by and helping him
Through times of pain and sorrow

His brothers and sisters are here
Spreading love and strength around
And his nieces and nephews wait
To share the food provided
His aunts are sitting silently
Anchors for truths that fly tonight

This is hard; this is real hard!

8 December 1990,
at Aswinis

When Worlds Collide

It hasn't been exactly productive
This week
My knees really ache sometimes
I never really did much at all.
When the weather changes
Just cleaned up some gold castings
Might quit playing basketball
I haven't been motivated for awhile
Hang up my runners this year

I hate to admit but I think
Time to change gears
I've finally begun to feel
I want to take up something new
Not old age, but just middle aged
I'd like to learn to sing and dance
It's kind of embarrassing.
It would be easier on
My knees

I want you to teach me to sing
It's the least I can do
I want you to show me how to dance
To help the cause
The dance has to be simple
Kitimat's pretty much dead
I want to start with the frontlet dance
Someone's got to start somewhere

Summer 1990,
in Vancouver

The Eagle

"Do you want an eagle?"
Two young boys asked me today.
I saw wrinkled song-leaders,
Waving magic wands for singers to see,
Tailfeathers.

I remembered men planted firmly atop
A chair, a stool, a platform,
Cheeks painted red,
Mouths gaping open,
Eyes squinted,
Heads tilted back,
Powerfully waving eagle tailfeathers
So others could sing songs.

I saw a thousand headdresses
Lying cold on metal museum shelves,
In a thousand different towns,
Collecting
dust,
Nothing else.
I pictured dignitaries bowing and swaying,
Dipping their heads
In time to songs,
Bobbing, stabbing, gliding,
Eagle down floating from crowns
Worn thousands of times by many
Generations.

When they returned with the eagle,
I took it from the sack
And stared . . .
Its feathers were ruffled and
Dirty looking.
A wing flopped.
Blood dripped.
Eyes stared.
It stunk all over.
Death.

Pulling long tapered feathers,
I saw an eagle soaring.
I pictured his beak ripping flesh.
Beauty?

One of the boys drowned in a puddle.

Spring 1985,
at Maaktosiis

From A UBC Library Window

Straight down
The green of the lawn is mottled
Patterned too by the branches and
Trunk of a naked tree

Just farther, a solitary crow
Rides atop another tree
That one still clothed in amber
Then a grove of manicured
Decorative oranges and rusty browns

Two concrete towers jump up
With white curtain teeth
So bright
Behind them, deep smokey blue
Mountains, mountains, mount . . .
Patchworked by logging, I presume.

Blanketing dirty grey fog
Soft clouds opening
Here and there, sky blue
Strokes of powder blue interrupt

Farther away still
Marching clouds lean
One onto another

Darker blue above
The off white clouds, shifting

A breeze begins to change all this.

Fall 1989,
in Vancouver

I Miss My Home This Exact Minute

When people gather to sing their songs,
And do their dances,
It is at these times,
That I miss my family the most.

When dark skies come,
And short days return,
And the smell of rain thickens,
I miss the wind blowing up river.

I picture familiar faces at the feast.
I can see brown necks swelling,
Pregnant with songs to sing.
Bodies crowd close, making room for others.

I think about my sister's potlatch.
She's naming her children,
Maybe this exact minute.
And I miss my home.

> *10 November 1990,*
> *at UBC, for my*
> *sister April, who named*
> *her children today*

Ron Hamilton: "A Biography of Sorts"

I was born and raised at Aswinis, on the West Coast of Vancouver Island. My mother was Nessie Watts, my father Clifford Hamilton. Through my mother, I trace my roots to the following groups: Huupachesath, Tsishaa-ath, and Hiikuulthath. Through my father to: Huupachesath, Aktiisath, and Waalas Kwaaqyuulth. I am connected by blood to members of every West Coast tribe.

As a youth, I was impressed by the creative skills of countless relatives, on both sides of my family, as our lives were connected and we crossed paths from time to time. The elderly took their role as teachers quite seriously, and some of them executed story-telling as skilfully as any published author today. Among those I considered the best and influential to me were: Ayaat — my mother's aunt, Chaamaat — my mother's brother, Ivan — my elder brother, George Clutesi — my parental uncle, Auntie Lizzy — my mother's elder sister, Walter Elliotte — my elder sister's husband's father's brother, and, most significantly, Mama — my mother. She used to say, "I'm not going to quit talking until I die." I was the last person to see my mother before she died, and she kept my attention during that visit by telling stories.

In my later youth, I had the great good fortune to share stories with an ever-widening circle of relatives, some of them living in villages different from my own. Among this secondary, though just as important, group of "teachers" were: Auntie Dimp — my father's younger sister, Auntie Vi — my father's older sister, Uncle Bennet — my father's brother, Maanikin — my father's uncle, Chixchin — my father's uncle, Larry Sport — my mother's cousin, Mary Moses — my mother's aunt, and Alec Williams — my mother's cousin's husband.

In addition to story-tellers, among my teachers along creative veins were many individuals recognized in our community as composers, singers, dancers, painters, sculptors, actors, and formal speakers. I would be disrespectful not to mention these: Nanny Kate, singer/dancer — my mother's aunt; Jacob Gallic, historian/singer — my mother's elder sister's husband (also

100

my eldest son's namesake); Peter Webster, composer/songleader — my mother's cousin; Billy Yukum, dancer/singer — my mother's cousin; Effie Tate, historian — my parental grandfather's cousin; Ida Jones, historian — my parental grandfather's cousin; Master Touchie, painter — my mother's cousin's husband; Cecil Mack, dancer/singer — my parental grandfather's cousin; Earnie Chester, singer/speaker/painter — my Hiik-uulthath cousin; Joe Smith, speaker — my parental grandfather's cousin; Jimmy Codfish, sculptor — my parental grandfather's uncle; John Jacobson, actor/music historian/philosopher/sculptor — my most active and intense mentor.

All of the above-mentioned individuals, with the exception of Walter Elliotte, a Cowichan, are from my own community on the West Coast. I received, as well, in my youth, public schooling to the eighth grade. One single teacher from this period stands out, far and above all others, for having shown me some consideration. He was Art Olson, my grade 8 English teacher, and not insignificantly a vocal fan of coastal Indian carving and painting. He'd taught in an up-coast village and recalled to our class several anecdotes, extolling the virtues of craftsmen and athletes he'd known personally. I always felt he was teaching for more than just a salary. He never once made me feel that I didn't belong in the public school system — others often did.

The University of British Columbia is not a particularly welcoming institution; however, a few individuals do stand out from the uniform grey of this foreboding establishment. Dr. Marjorie Halpin has consistently encouraged me to work diligently at my writing — to craft it. She has also made me understand not only that do I have something to offer the world through my writing but also that there are many waiting to read what native authors have to share with the outside world. As well, Jane Flick, of the English Department, gave me good, honest, and constructive criticism on the papers I wrote for her while I was in her "Introduction to Canadian Literature" class. When the last class of the course was over, she generously gave me an old typewriter, explaining that her father had used it throughout his university career, and that she had done the same. As I left her office carrying the typewriter, she said, "I know you'll put it to good use."

In non-Indian Canadian society, an individual's school experience is looked at to determine something about the individual. In my community, who one's relations are and what roles one plays in one's extended family say much about who one is. Names, sometimes passed down through inheritance for many generations, take great significance. At the expressed request of the editors of this volume, the following is a partial list of the names given to me in our potlatch system to date:

Hapkwachuu — "Hair all over," "Covered with hair." This name was given to me by my mother when I was a boy. It is something like a nick-name, and it was the first Indian name I was given.

Kwaawiina — "Raven" in the Kwaakwaala language. This name last be-longed to my parental grandfather's younger brother, Robert George of the Huupachesath tribe. Its source was the Waalas Kwaaqyuulth via Kyu-quot. After my father was buried a feast was held that evening, and it was then that my great uncle, Tommy Hunt, and his son, George, performed the Haamaatsa. Two of my brothers and I were named then. I was given this name on that occasion by my late parental aunt, Grace Watts of the Tsishaa-ath tribe.

Kwayis — "Something else," "Source of unusual births." This name was given to me during a TluuKwaana "wolf" ceremony, held in the Skway-maalt big house around the winter of 1969-1970. The host was Andrew Callikum, and he was the one who gave me this name. His parental grand-father was my parental grandfather's uncle.

Wuuyaakiihtuu — "Someone very special." This name was given to me by my parental great-aunt, Sophie Jules, wife of Chief Kapchaa, both late of Huupsitas, on the occasion of the memorial potlatch they hosted for their son, David, in the early 1980s.

Kwayatsapaalth — "Carrying a wolf on the back," "Owning a wolf." This name was given to me by my parental great-aunt, Josephine Tom, in 1979, at Victoria, on the occasion of her potlatch in honour of her late husband, Chief Mike Tom Sr. Josephine's father, "Captain Jack," held this name formerly at Yuquot.

Sha'tsiiyakib — "The one arm that holds up the world." My parental great-aunt gave me this name on the occasion of a great potlatch, held in Balaatsad, to pass various ceremonial rights on to the next generation of her family. Chief Kelly Peters, her husband, was the source of the name.

Tlaakwaaqiikamay — "Copper Chief." This title, actually the name of a seat, formerly held by my parental grandfather, was passed down to me by my parental great-aunt, Cecilia John, and Kwishmaats, on the occasion of the marriage of her daughter, Caroline, to his son, Billy Oskar, in the early 1980s.

Ki-ke-in — "Long sounding thunder." This name was given to me by my mother's elder sister, my Auntie Lizzy Gallic. Formerly my maternal great-great-grandfather, head chief of the Hiikuulthath tribe, held the name. In 1983 I gave a potlatch to name my two eldest sons, and it was on that occasion that she bestowed the name on me.

Tliitlaalaadzii — "Big fire that never dies down." I received this name from my parental great-uncle, Chief Alvin Alfred, at the last-mentioned potlatch. He had received it from his uncle, Chief Dan Cranmer, of the Nimpkish people.

Tlaaliis — "Always a big whale on the beach." From Chief Alvin Alfred, at my 1983 potlatch. The name was formerly his personal name.

Hwunhwilaas — "Where the thunder comes from." This name was given to me on the occasion of my 1983 potlatch by my approximately 100-year-old great-aunt, Aaxua, Chief Alvin Alfred's mother.

Hiilthaamas — "He fixes everything," "He makes everything right." Chief Jimmy Sewide, my parental great-aunt Flora's husband, and author of *Guests Never Leave Hungry*, gave me this name on the occasion of the 1983 potlatch to name my sons.

Tlaatsatsum — "He feasts the people with whale blubber." Chief Bob Martin of the Tla-o-qui-aht people, my parental uncle, gave me this name, along with a beautifully crafted traditional West Coast canoe, the handiwork of himself and his sons, on the occasion of his potlatch to name his children. I had, with much help from Lyle Wilson, of Kitimat, painted Chief Martin's family crest curtain for the event.

Chuu,
Ki-ke-in
(Ron Hamilton)
at Musqueam,
Winter 1991

A Study of Education in Context*

E. RICHARD ATLEO

"In marked contrast to the historical emphasis upon Euro-Canadian decision making and authority over Indian education dating back to the 'discovery' of America, today's Indian pupils, particularly in British Columbia, may now attend schools whose entire governance is in the hands of their own parents and relatives."

*   *   *

In 1949 there were sixteen British Columbia status Indians enrolled in grade 12. By 1985 this enrolment had risen 31.5 times to 505. Over the same time, the British Columbia status Indian on-reserve population had risen from 23,881 to 39,067, a 1.6 fold increase. Thus, proportionally speaking, the increase in grade 12 enrolments is considerably greater than the increase in the population from which the grade 12 students are drawn. The problem is to provide a plausible explanation for this apparent change in enrolment since 1949.

The reason for this examination is that grade 12 enrolment patterns have apparently changed so recently that as late as 1976, Brooks observed that "studies examining the academic achievement of Indian children yield what is now a familiar and dreary statistic. Clearly, we have not been successful in this regard, yet there are few answers available" (p. 192). In 1967 Hawthorn reported one "dreary statistic," in a national survey of Canada's Indians, as a 94 percent failure rate. That is, the grade 12 enrolment of 1961 was 6 percent of the grade 1 enrolment of 1949. In British Columbia (the focus of this study), the indicated failure rate of Indian pupils for the same period was 96 percent. That is, according to Hawthorn's method of calculation the grade 12 enrolment in British Columbia was 4 percent of the grade 1 enrolment of eleven years previous. Hawthorn's figures, for Canadian society in general, showed a failure rate of

---

* In his second article for this collection (for the first, and for a profile of him, see pp. 48-61) Dr. Atleo provides an extract from his doctoral dissertation which discusses the very important issue of education policy as it relates to the heritage of the First Nations.

only 12 percent. The observed large increase in the grade 12 enrolment pattern of status Indians in British Columbia between 1949 and 1985 requires that an up-to-date analysis be performed.

To set the stage for an updated analysis, it is useful to examine how Hawthorn and others explained the Indian educational failure which they observed. This explanation leads to an explanation of the theory of context.

Explanations of Indian Educational Failure and a Theory of Context

In the past, the most common theoretical explanations of Indian educational failure focused on the differences of culture, broadly speaking, between the Indian and non-Indian (Erickson, 1987; Ogbu, 1987). Indian pupils fail in school, it was initially maintained, because of cultural deprivation. Since there are a variety of definitions of culture, this paper will assume that one culture may be defined by contrasting it with another culture. Lévi-Strauss (1963) wrote of such contrasts as "significant discontinuities." For example, the group-oriented values of one group may be said to be a significant discontinuity from the individually oriented values of another group. The former group places a higher value on group goals, while the latter group places a higher value upon individual goals. The general definition of culture by Lévi-Strauss has the advantage of not being bound by a specific context and may be applied to comparative cultures even as they change and evolve.

Historically, in Indian-white relations, the task of defining culture meant references to language differences, belief differences, behavioural differences, skin colour differences, and so on, but today these differences seem to have evolved into a degree of uniformity and to have become blurred in some cases. Some Indians today may speak only English, hold similar beliefs to those of non-Indians, behave in a fashion similar to non-Indians, and even have a skin colour that is not distinguishable from non-Indians. Yet "significant discontinuities" between the Indian and others are implied in the use of the phrase "Indian culture," even when some of the formerly significant discontinuities such as language and beliefs may not be as significant as they were in the past.

Nevertheless, if historical roots are considered part of culture, then an Indian culture is certainly different from other cultures whose historical roots may be from other lands. The importance of historical roots is based upon the assumption that fundamental beliefs about life are transferred from one generation to another. Moreover, when the fundamental beliefs about life become assumptions of culture which are not usually articulated

(Lane, 1967), the transfer becomes automatic and largely unconscious. It is perhaps in the area of the assumptions of culture rooted in the distant past that the Indian of today may differ even if other cultural differences seem to be blurring into "insignificant continuities" as opposed to "significant discontinuities."

During the 1950s the perception that Indians had an impoverished culture was of course an historical legacy of European notions of cultural superiority. Hence, it was theorized that because the Indian was impoverished in culture he or she must begin school with an apparently insurmountable handicap. "Impoverished in culture" referred to a lack of Euro-Canadian culture within the Indian. Hawthorn reported that, during the 1950s, non-Indians did not expect Indians in general to develop socially acceptable skills along the same lines as whites. The implication was that the Indian lacked the meanings of Euro-Canadian culture and this type of impoverishment led to maladaptive social behaviour, Indian educational failure, and so on.

Then it was thought during the 1960s that Indians did not have an impoverished culture after all, and so the reason for their lack of achievement in school was now thought to be caused by cultural discontinuity (Hawthorn, 1967; Ogbu, 1987). Leslie Gue (1974) characterized cultural discontinuity in terms of value differences. For example, the Indian may hold group goals as being more important than individual goals, while the non-Indian may hold individual goals to be more important than group goals. Both held the same range of goal values, but each put a different focus or emphasis upon these goal values depending upon what was considered more important.

Subsequent explanations of Indian educational failure are variants of this cultural discontinuity perspective. More (1986), for example, suggests that Indian pupils in general have different learning styles from others. Learning styles are culturally determined. Therefore, an Indian pupil encountering an alien learning style in a classroom suffers cultural discontinuity. More's perspective is strengthened by other observations of remarkable and basic differences between the Indian worldview and western man's worldview. DeFaveri (1984) holds that the Indian worldview is characterized by oneness with the universe while the western worldview is characterized by individualism and isolationism. The former worldview holds that everything is related and connected in some way, while the latter worldview may recognize holistic subsystems within the universe yet tend to the opposite view that reality is not necessarily made up of related or connected parts. Brumbaugh (1963, p. 136), philosophizing about this phenomenon in education, has said that while the "separations [of reality] are useful, even vital" they have been overdone and "ignore the basic character of the experiential continuum." In contrast to the separations of reality which might be argued to be characteristic of the western world-view, the Indian worldview is characterized by wholeness, connectedness, and interrelationships (Kluckhohn, 1949; Bryde, 1971; Sealy, 1973; De-Faveri, 1984; Berger, 1985; Friesen, 1985; Kelly & Nelson, 1986; Mc-Caskill, 1987). More's suggestion, therefore, is that teachers of Indian pupils should attempt to suit their teaching style to the Indian learning style, which has been affected by assumptions of the wholeness and inter-relatedness of reality.

It is no great step to move from the view that a minority culture is different to the view that the minority group is genetically inferior. A theoretical view of genetic inferiority formed part of the rationale for the "impoverished in culture" view of the 1950s (Erickson, 1987) and dropped into disuse as such views became unacceptable in the seventies. It has recently resurfaced, however, in the view that the Indian is right-brained and therefore deficient in language function. Chrisjohn and Lanigan (1986) assert that no reliable data exist "to conclude that such a deficit is indeed present in Indians" (p. 55). In another paper Chrisjohn and Peters (1986) draw the following conclusions:

We suggest that the neurological and neuropsychological evidence is nowhere near conclusive at this point, and that the performance patterns of Native American children do not necessarily reflect a "right brain dominance" of the Native Americans. As of now, the "right brained Indian" has to be considered a myth rather than a scientifically valid fact. (p. 62)

It could, of course, be argued that other pupils from different cultural backgrounds have entered the Canadian school system, apparently with the same kinds of handicaps as the Indian, and have not failed as completely as the Indian has failed, and that therefore it is reasonable to assume that if no other plausible explanations about Indian educational failure are available then the possibility that the Indian is genetically inferior may be entertained. The present study does not accept this argument and examines the possibility of a plausible perspective other than that of genetic inferiority to account for Indian educational failure.

This perspective of Indian educational failure views it from a theory of context. This theory assumes that there is a relationship between an individual and the society in which that individual lives. If the relationship is characterized by a negative orientation of society towards that individual, then the theory of context holds that that individual will be negatively affected. For example, if society rejects an individual socially, politically, and economically, then that individual may respond by committing suicide, behaving in unacceptable and deviant ways in order to survive, or by emigrating to another country if possible. On the other hand, the theory of context holds that when society accepts an individual socially, politically, and economically, then that individual may respond by behaving in socially acceptable ways. The assumed relationship between an individual and society is also argued to apply, in general, to the relationship between society and a minority group.

An important aspect of the theory of context is that it forces a shift in the focus of any discussion about Indian educational failure from the differences between the Indian and non-Indian to a focus upon similarities between the Indian and non-Indian. Where the focus was formerly on "significant discontinuities" between the Indian and non-Indian, it is now on what may be termed "significant continuities." Although the Indian and non-Indian may differ culturally in terms of historical roots and in terms of special legislation about Indians, they are nevertheless similar in other respects. For example, they share the same country and form parts of the same Canadian society. Whether Indians profess an affinity for western civilization or not, they nevertheless demonstrate a tacit acceptance, at least of its material benefits, by living in modern homes, driving modern cars, and generally enjoying all the modern conveniences. In addition, many Indians can be found participating in society today in a variety of unskilled, skilled, and even professional jobs, attending schools whose curriculum is mainly Euro-Canadian, attending various Christian churches, taking advantage of modern recreational facilities, and generally striving to do well within rather than without Canadian society. Even those Indians who may openly reject western ways and values can find no escape from minimal participation in Canadian society by their need for money, medical aid, and so on.

Yet in spite of the tacit acceptance and the apparent similarities between the two groups, the Indian position in Canadian society is more of a propinquitous than a volitional nature. European civilization came to North America by colonization and thus became an inevitable and fixed context for the local Indian. The position of the Indian in such a case is referred to as an involuntary one by Ogbu (1987). It is an involuntary position within Canadian society in the sense that the Indian's minority position was, and is, not by choice. Involuntary minorities are thus contrasted with voluntary minorities who immigrate. Ogbu found that voluntary minorities tend to do well in school, in contrast with involuntary minorities who tend not to do well. He cites such examples as the Buraku minority in Japan who do poorly in school but do well when they emigrate to the United States; the minority Koreans in Japan who do poorly in school but who do well when they emigrate to the United States; the Mexicans born in the United States who do poorly in school while their brothers born in Mexico tend to do well when they emigrate to the United States.

Gibson (1987) also found, in a case study of first-generation immigrant Punjabi pupils in California, that they tended to do well in school even in the face of social and linguistic difficulties. These and other like studies are said to indicate a relationship between the voluntary and involuntary nature of minorities and their academic achievement and failure. What is brought to the fore by such interpretations is the consideration of the relationship among the individual, society, and the education system. John Dewey (1938) said that the purpose of education is not only to "graduate out of" school but also to "graduate into" a meaningful society. Dewey's stated purpose of education is for a student to graduate out of a local school into a larger society which, rather than providing insurmountable challenges and opportunities, says to the graduate "you have a place with us if we find you acceptable and you find us acceptable."

In such a case, where society and student-graduate find themselves mutually acceptable, it may be said that the student has graduated into a meaningful context. Dosman (1972) would define this relationship between an individual and society as inclusion. As the word suggests, inclusion refers to an acceptance by the dominant society of an individual or minority group. Exclusion is therefore the opposite and indicates a form of rejection by a dominant society of an individual or minority group. In the case of exclusion, society may now say to the graduate, "you have no place with us because we do not find you acceptable even if you find us acceptable."

Another author, Adler (1982), maintains that when minority students can see no hope of securing meaningful jobs for themselves through education they will not be motivated to work hard or to do well in school, because they see no purpose in graduating into a society which offers no hope of meaningful or gainful employment. What Dewey and Adler may refer to as a meaningless context because of rejection by a dominant society seem to be the same conditions as those which Frideres (1974) calls racism against a minority and Dosman (1972) exclusion. That is, when the majority culture or society engages in various means of oppression such as refusing access to quality education, refusing access to good jobs, refusing access to political opportunities and so on, such activity may be perceived by the minority as racism and exclusion which may contribute to their perception of the larger society as being an oppressively meaningless context.

Although Barman, Hebert & McCaskill (1986, 1987) would agree that Indian educational failure is an unfortunate Canadian legacy, they would also agree that changes are currently taking place in Indian communities. These changes are perceived as part of a worldwide movement of colonized people everywhere demanding freedom from, and equality with, their colonial masters, and it may or may not be significant that these changes taking place in Canadian Indian communities coincide with increasing grade 12 enrolments among British Columbia status Indian students.

This demand for freedom in Canada is being expressed as a demand for a form of self-government by Indian people. Although Indian self-government is still an unresolved constitutional issue, one of its expressions is Indian control of Indian education (Adams, 1974; CEA Report, 1984; Cummins, 1985; Barman, Hebert & McCaskill, 1986, 1987; Battiste, 1987; Diamond, 1987; Douglas, 1987), the definition of which also remains an issue. Nevertheless, Indian control of Indian education is finding an expression in practice where educational decisions formerly made by others may now be made by Indian people.

In marked contrast to the historical emphasis upon Euro-Canadian decision-making and authority over Indian education dating back to the "discovery" of America, today's Indian pupils, particularly in British Columbia, may now attend schools whose entire governance is in the hands of their own parents and relatives. Where Indian pupils formerly looked to non-Indian administrators for educational direction, they may now look to their own parents, who may be involved as members of the Indian school board, or as Indian principals, Indian teachers, Indian school counsellors, or as Indian political leaders, for educational direction. In 1987, an Indian Affairs computer printout indicated that 184 bands out of 196 in British Columbia had decided to assume control over some or all of their educational programs. There is considerable variety in these programs. The range includes one Indian-controlled provincial public school district (School District No. 92), twenty-six Indian-controlled elementary schools, ten elementary-secondary schools, and fifty-two Indian-controlled kindergarten-nursery schools located on reserve. Although not completely staffed by Indians, and perhaps deliberately so, all of these educational programs are definitely marked by Indian decision-making. Such educational systems, by and large, have remained essentially Euro-Canadian in terms of organizational behaviour and organizational structure, as well as in curriculum content, but those in authority over the structure and content have changed.

In sum, this discussion of explanations of Indian educational failure suggests an examination of Indian education in terms of a theory of context, not so much because traditional theories are necessarily incorrect, for traditional theories do provide some reasonable rationale for Indian educational failure, but because traditional theories are based upon the assumption that the only source for possible answers, as determined by the dominant society, is found in the object of educational failure. For example, the traditional theory of cultural deprivation emphasizes the importance of Euro-Canadian culture and devalues the importance of Indian culture. That is, this theory does not entertain the possibility that part of the answer to Indian educational failure may lie in the value of Indian culture for Indian people. The theory of cultural discontinuity and its variants are inadequate explanations of Indian educational failure for basically the same reason. By contrast, the theory of context allows us to seek explanations for failure (and, of course, success) in the nature of the relationship between a dominant and a minority society rather than in the inability or unwillingness of one group to conform to the imposed values of another.

Based upon the perspective of the theory of context, the following hypothesized relationship is proposed. Inclusion (social, political, and economic) is expected to be positively associated with academic achievement as measured by increasing enrolment into grade 12 while exclusion (social, political, and economic) is expected to be associated with no increases in academic achievement as measured by enrolment into grade 12.

Research Method and Design

This is an ex post facto study of archival data. These data are of two kinds, the first amenable to statistical treatment, the second not so amenable. The first kind of data consists of the numbers of status Indians in British Columbia enrolled in grade 12 each year from 1949 to 1985. The second is the indicators of contextual conditions, external and internal to schools. The combination of quantitative and qualitative data analysis identifies the study design as a marriage of two research approaches. Empirical data is analyzed within a qualitative context. While it is easy to see the grade 12 enrolments as the dependent variable in such a study, it is not so easy to see the contextual conditions as independent variables as in a true quasi experimental study. For this reason, the terms "dependent variable" and "independent variable" are avoided.

A major assumption of this study is that a society may have distinctive prevailing characteristics that can be identified. Identification may be based upon views that are commonly held and actions that are widely practised in that society. For example, if it is commonly held by a dominant society that Indians are "lazy" and if, at the same time, employers of that dominant society, in general, refuse to hire Indians (Hawthorn, 1967) then that dominant society may be said to have the distinctive characteristic of prejudice which is manifested by the practice of economic exclusion.

Another major assumption is that enrolment into grade 12 equates with academic achievement. This assumption includes the implication that the students are in the normal grade 12 age range in an academic grade 12 class as opposed to an alternate or special grade 12 class.

Analysis of the Provincial Enrolment Data

In this section are presented first the raw data on grade 12 enrolments of status Indians, second the results of applying time-series analysis to the raw data, and, finally, an analysis of cumulative enrolments and periodic averages.

The Raw Data

The presentation in figure 1 on page 113 represents the grade 12 enrolments of B.C. status Indians from 1949 to 1985 in proportion to the on-reserve populations over the same time. In order to examine the apparent trend in the graph, the data were subjected to a time-series analysis.

The Analysis

The average proportional change in grade 12 enrolment between 1949 and 1981 was .0003363 students. If the average change is calculated for each successive year it will be found that the estimated average grade 12 enrolment change during the 1950s ranges between seven and ten students, while during the 1960s and 1970s it ranges between eleven and thirteen.

The years 1982-1983, in contrast, yield an estimated and significant increase of .0003320 over and above the estimated average of .0003363. This represents an estimated change of twenty five students for 1982 and 1983. From 1949 to 1981 grade 12 enrolments varied in its average yearly change by seven to thirteen students. Then in 1982 and 1983 the average yearly enrolment change jumped to an average of twenty-five students.

Analysis of Cumulative and Average Figures

Although the time-series analysis shows statistically significant enrolment increases and a statistically significant intervention effect, it is felt that an

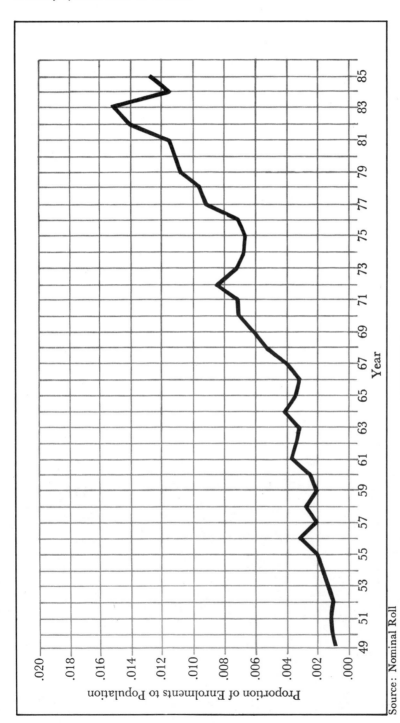

Source: Nominal Roll

FIGURE 1

Grade 12 Enrolments of Status Indians in British Columbia, 1949-1985

TABLE 1

Grade 12 Status Indian Enrolment in Proportion to the On Reserve Population in British Columbia: 1949 to 1985

Year	Grade 12 Enrolment	On-Reserve Population	Proportion Enrol/pop
1949	16	23,881	.00067
1950	24	22,857*	.00105
1951	30	22,222	.00135
1952	23	23,958*	.00096
1953	32	24,060*	.00133
1954	42	25,926	.00162
1955	57	26,147*	.00218
1956	84	26,087*	.00322
1957	49	26,064*	.00188
1958	69	26,135*	.00264
1959	60	30,869	.00194
1960	75	31,962*	.00235
1961	120	33,083*	.00363
1962	114	34,164*	.00334
1963	114	35,281*	.00323
1964	155	36,272*	.00427
1965	132	37,256	.00354
1966	112	35,081	.00319
1967	140	33,474	.00418
1968	171	33,061	.00517
1969	195	32,157	.00606
1970	232	32,573	.00712
1971	232	32,496	.00714
1972	288	33,339	.00864
1973	241	33,702	.00715
1974	226	33,617	.00672
1975	220	33,060	.00665
1976	230	33,164	.00694
1977	312	33,888	.00921
1978	324	33,717	.00961
1979	366	34,204	.01070
1980	384	34,807	.01103
1981	408	35,704	.01143
1982	526	36,895	.01426
1983	578	38,002	.01521
1984	441	38,673	.01140
1985	505	39,067	.01293

Note: the * indicates interpolations for the years when a census was not taken. Each interpolation is an estimated average between the known populations. Also, the on-reserve populations for 1949, 1951 and 1954 are estimated from on-off reserve totals.

alternative method of analysis may help to support, strengthen, and further clarify the significance of the results of the time-series analysis. The alternative method proposed involves an analysis of cumulative enrolments and periodic averages as shown in Table 2.

TABLE 2

Cumulative Grade 12 Enrolments (academic years): 1949-1985

1949-1961	1961-1973	1973-1985
561	2005	4256

24 year average = 1283 per 12 years vs 4256 per 12 years

The cumulative total for the first 24 years, 1949 to 1973, is 2,566 grade 12 students, while the cumulative total for the final 12 years is 4,256. If the first 24-year cumulative grade 12 enrolment total is averaged, the result is 1,283 students per 12-year period. Therefore the final 12-year cumulative total of 4,256 grade 12 students is 3.32 times more than the average of the first 24-year cumulative grade 12 enrolment. Although no specific statistical significance is attached to these numbers they do help to clarify, for those who have only used, hitherto, the ordinary least squares method of analysis, the nature of the enrolment trend by roughly confirming where the greatest areas of significance occurred.

Discussion: Hypothesized Relationships with Context

It was predicted that inclusion (social, political, and economic) was associated positively with academic achievement as measured by increasing grade 12 enrolments. The time-series analysis indicated that the grade 12 enrolment pattern did show significant increases between 1949 and 1985. The agreement between the cumulative grade 12 enrolment data and the results of the time-series analysis is in the placement of the greatest number of enrollees in the enrolment series. Both types of analysis place the greatest number of grade 12 enrollees in the final 12-year period between 1974 and 1985. Since the final 12-year period overlaps the 1970s and 1980s, which have been identified as the periods of relative inclusivity, the prediction that there is a positive association between academic achievement as measured by increasing grade 12 enrolments and contextual inclusivity is tentatively supported by both the cumulative enrolment data and the time-series analysis.

Moreover, the first 12 years in the enrolment series record the lowest grade 12 enrolments, and this finding is associated with the identification of the 1950s as being more exclusive than the 1960s. Similarly the 1960s, which is identified as a period of transition, with elements of inclusion in it not found during the 1950s, is related to the relatively higher grade 12 enrolments as recorded in the second 12-year period shown in Table 3 below. The assumption here is that the higher grade 12 enrolments of the 1960s are related to the inclusive elements of the period rather than to the exclusive elements. The table associates the social orientations of each time period with the cumulative grade 12 enrolment total of those periods in order to show the associations between them.

TABLE 3

Cumulative Grade 12 Enrolments in 12 Academic Year Periods: 1949-1985 in Relation to the Social Orientation of Each Period

1949-1961	1961-1973	1973-1985
Exclusive	Transitional	Inclusive
561	2005	4256

In conclusion, the theory of context may be said to be tentatively supported. Since the completion of this study, the theory of context has been found to be useful in other areas. For example, in the issue of repatriation of cultural heritage where historical conditions must be taken into account, the theory of context provides a model by which sound policy may be developed.

BIBLIOGRAPHY

Adams, D. (1974). "Self-Determination and Indian education: A case study." Journal of American Indian Education. 13, (2), 21-27.

Adler, Mortimer J. (1982). The Paideia Proposal: An Educational Manifesto. New York: Collier Books, Macmillan Publishing Company.

Barman, J., Hebert, Y. M. & McCaskill, D. (1986). "The legacy of the past: An overview." In Barman, J., Hebert, Y. M. & McCaskill, D. (Eds.), Indian Education in Canada: Vol. 1. The legacy, 1-21. Vancouver, B.C.: University of British Columbia Press.

——— (1987). "The challenge of Indian education: An overview." In Barman, J., Hebert, Y. M. & McCaskill, D. (Eds.), Indian Education in Canada: Vol. 2. The challenge, 1-21. Vancouver, B.C.: University of British Columbia Press.

Battiste, M. (1986). "Micmac literacy and cognitive assimilation." In Barman, J., Hebert, Y. M. & McCaskill, D. (Eds.), Indian Education in Canada: Vol. 1. The legacy, 23-44. Vancouver, B.C.: University of British Columbia Press.

———— (1987). "Mi'Kmaq linguistic integrity: A case study of Mi'Kmawey School." In Barman, J., Hebert, Y. M. & McCaskill, D. (Eds.), Indian Education in Canada: Vol. 2. The challenge, 107-25. Vancouver, B.C.: University of British Columbia Press.

Berger, Thomas (1979). Native Rights in the New World: A Glance at History. Speech given at the Empress Hotel, Victoria, B.C. (December 4th).

———— (1985). Village Journey: The Report of the Alaska Native Review Commission. New York: Hill and Wang.

Brooks, I. R. (1976). Native Education in Canada and the United States: A Bibliography. University of Calgary: Office of Educational Development.

Brumbaugh, R. S. & Lawrence, N. M. (1963). Philosophers on Education: Six Essays on the Foundations of Western Thought. Boston: Houghton Mifflin Company.

Bryde, John F. (1971). Modern Indian Psychology. Vermillion, South Dakota: Institute of Indian Studies, The University of South Dakota.

CEA Report (1984). Recent Developments in Native Education. Toronto, Ontario: Canadian Education Association.

Chrisjohn, R. D., & Lanigan, C. B. (1986). "Research on Indian intelligence testing: Review and prospects." A paper prepared for Mokakit Indian Education Research Association, 50-57. Vancouver, B.C.

Chrisjohn, R. D. & Peters, M. (1986). "The right brained Indian: Fact or fiction?" Canadian Journal of Native Education, 13 (1), 62-71.

DeFaveri, Ivan (1984). "Contemporary ecology and traditional native thought." Canadian Journal of Native Education, 12, (1), 1-9.

Dewey, John (1938). Experience and Education. New York: Collier Books.

Diamond, B. (1987). "The Cree experience." In Barman, J., Hebert, Y. M. & McCaskill, D. (Eds.), Indian Education in Canada: Vol. 2. The challenge, 86-106. Vancouver, B.C.: University of British Columbia Press.

Dosman, Edgar (1972). Indians: The Urban Dilemma. Toronto: McClelland and Stewart Limited.

Douglas, V. R. (1987). "The education of urban native children: The Sacred Circle Project." In Barman, J., Hebert, Y. M. & McCaskill, D. (Eds.), Indian Education in Canada: Vol. 2. The challenge, 180-209. Vancouver, B.C.: University of British Columbia Press.

Erickson, Frederick (1987). "Transformation and school success: The politics and culture of educational achievement." Anthropology and Education Quarterly, 18, (4), 335-56.

Frideres, James S. (1974). Canada's Indians: Contemporary Conflicts. Scarborough, Ontario: Prentice Hall.

Friesen, John W. (1985). When Cultures Clash: Case Studies in Multiculturalism. Calgary, Alberta: Detselig Enterprises Limited.

Gibson, Margaret A. (1987). "The school performance of immigrant minorities: A comparative view." Anthropology and Education Quarterly, 18, (4), 262-75.

Government of Canada (1959). Indian Registered Population by Sex and Residence. Ottawa: Indian and Northern Affairs Canada. (Also 1960 to 1986 issues)

———— (1973). Estimates of Vital Rates for the Canadian Indians: 1960-1970. By Victor Piche, Department of Demography, Montreal and M. V. George, Demographic Analysis and Research Section, Census Division Statistics Canada, Ottawa.

———— (1976). Indian Education Nominal — 1970 Roll System. Ottawa: Indian And Northern Affairs Canada.

———— (1981a). The Canadian Constitution 1981. Ottawa: Government of Canada.

———— (1981b). Indian Acts and Amendments, 1868-1950. Ottawa: Indian and Northern Affairs Canada.

———— (1981c). Contemporary Indian Legislation, 1951-1978. Ottawa: Indian and Northern Affairs Canada.

———— (1981d). British Columbia Indian Treaties in Historical Perspective. Ottawa: Indian and Northern Affairs Canada.

———— (1981e). 1980-1981 Program Review: Department of Indian Affairs, B.C. Region. Vancouver, B.C.: Indian and Northern Affairs Canada. (Also 1982-1983 Program Review)

———— (1981f). Annual Report 1980-1981. Ottawa: Indian and Northern Affairs Canada.

———— (1982). Indian Education Paper: Phase 1. Ottawa: Indian and Northern Affairs Canada.

———— (1983). Indian Self-Government in Canada: Report of the Special Committee. Ottawa: Indian and Northern Affairs Canada.

———— (1985). Background Notes to the First Ministers Conference: Canada's Aboriginal Peoples — Who They Are. Ottawa: Indian and Northern Affairs Canada.

———— (1985). Indian Act: R. S., c. 1-6 amended by c. 10 (2nd Supp.) 1974-75-76, c. 48: 1978-79, cc. 47, 110: 1984, cc. 40, 41: 1985, c. 27: August 1985. Ministry of Supply and Services Canada, 1985.

———— (1986). The Canadian Indian. Ottawa: Indian and Northern Affairs Canada.

———— (1988). INAC Education Program: British Columbia Region Administrative Handbook. Vancouver, B.C.: Indian and Northern Affairs Canada.

Gue, Leslie R. (1974). Indian Education in Canada. Department of Education Administration: The University of Alberta. Edmonton, Alta.

Hawthorn, H. B. (1966). A Survey of the Contemporary Indians of Canada. Vol. 1. Ottawa: Indian Affairs Branch.

———— (1967). A Survey of the Contemporary Indians of Canada. Vol. 2. Ottawa: Indian Affairs Branch.

Hawthorn, H. B., Belshaw, C. S., & Jamieson, S. M. (1958). The Indians of British Columbia: A Study of Contemporary Social Adjustment. Toronto: University of Toronto Press.

Kelly, M. L. & Nelson, C. H. (1986). "A nontraditional education model with Indian indigenous social service workers." Canadian Journal of Native Education, 13, (3), 42-55.

Kluckhohn, Clyde (1949). "The philosophy of the Navaho Indians." In Northrop, F. S. C. (Ed.). Ideological Differences and World Order, 356-84. New Haven & London: Yale University Press.

Lane, Barbara (1967). Aspects of Contemporary Indian Cultures with Emphasis on Implications for Teaching. Proceedings of Conference on the Indian Child and His Education. Extension Department of UBC.

Lévi-Strauss, Claude (1963). Structural Anthropology. New York: Basic Books, Inc.

McCaskill, D. (1987). "Revitalization of Indian culture: Indian cultural survival schools." In Barman, J., Hebert, Y. M. & McCaskill, D. (Eds.), Indian Education in Canada: Vol. 2. The challenge, 153-79. Vancouver, B.C.: University of British Columbia Press.

More, A. J. (1980). "Native Indian teacher education in Canada." Education Canada, 20, (1), 32-41.

———— (1984). Okanagan Nicola Indian Quality of Education Study. Penticton: Okanagan Indian Learning Institute.

———— (1986). Native Indian Students and Their Learning Styles: Research Results and Classroom Applications. Paper presented at an Indian Education Conference, Reno, Nevada.

More, A. J. & Wallis, J. H. (1979). Native Teacher Education: A Survey of Native Teacher Education Projects in Canada. Vancouver, B.C.: Canadian Indian Teacher Education Projects Conference.

More, A. J., MacDonald, L., Stringer, J., & Willey, T. (1983). Indian Education Projects and Programs in B.C. Schools. Vancouver, B.C.: University of British Columbia.

Ogbu, John U. (1987). "Variability in minority school performance: A problem in search of an explanation." Anthropology and Education Quarterly, 18, (4), 312-34.

Sealey, D. Bruce (1973a). "The settlement of the Americas." In Sealey, D. Bruce & Kirkness, Verna J. (Eds.). Indians Without Tipis: A Resource Book by Indians and Metis, 1-6. Winnipeg: William Clare (Manitoba) Limited.

———— (1973b). "Indians of Canada: An historical sketch." In Sealey, D. Bruce & Kirkness, Verna J. (Eds.). Indians Without Tipis: A Resource Book by Indians and Metis, 9-37. Winnipeg: William Clare (Manitoba) Limited.

———— (1973c). "Fish Lake: A case study." In Sealey, D. Bruce & Kirkness, Verna J. (Eds.). Indians Without Tipis: A Resource Book by Indians and Metis, 251-61. Winnipeg: William Clare (Manitoba) Limited.

Fourth World

Mechanical, performed by rote
Such schooled repetitions of thought
And offered to ignorant armies
Of twice lost seekers

1969 and Chrétien were authors?
And architects grand?
Creating a chorus of voices?
They tore our throats open for all to see?

We now have understandable songs?
And sing in your slop trough temples?
Every note is tailored to your scale?
Your speaker should mark my tempo?

Fourth World was authored by one of our
Own, a Shuswap, George Manuel.
He came from our soil and returned
And countless before raised arms to fight

A footnote in your dry mouth, *Fourth World*
Is warmed food in my hungry mind.

Summer 1985,
at Nuu-chah-nulth
Tribal Council meeting,
Hiitatsuu reserve

Michelle

At the university conference
"Indian Education Today"
White teachers from residential
And day schools discussed our lives

And a drunk Indian reverend
Danced his cannibal dance
Ashamed, he then put on
A white mask to preach

But Michelle you move young
And naive and brave and
Innocently honest
You . . . you stood erect

Your voice was sure
Your confidence obvious
Your mouth firm
Your thick round lips set proudly

The human colour of your complexion
Caught my eyes
And I turned to watch you talk,
To hear you show your mind

You spoke your own language
Straight and full of emotion
You spit your words in imitation
Of their style

You heated up the day
And showed many teachers themselves
Your cheeks glowed
Brown rounds against white walls

You were a residential school teacher
Talking Nicola, ignorant, rigid, domineering
Your straight black hair hung over
Your youthful shoulder, soft

And when your skit was done
You let them free of their guilt
Your every move was grace itself
Not calculated to have its effect

And when you were through acting
Your voice began to hum peacefully
And grew ever deeper
A natural resonance replaced its edge

Leaving the discussions we sought
Each other on the grass
And in the woods
Near magnificent decaying spirits

Inside the conference
You were the face of nature.
Outside, a supernatural power.
You were somehow too real to me

Your voice and way of talking
So peaceful and easy to remember
Carried me as far as you let it
I lost control and surrendered all

When you smiled your cheeks
Pulled up and creased the corners
Of your soft inviting eyes
Their black, the warmest colour I'd known.

We were meant to cross paths
To meet at this queer intersection
You knew that and moved so well
I didn't and walked like a newborn.

You took me to the park
And walked my legs off
You laughed so beautifully
I cried behind your back

And you quit school
For the movement and then the
Street
And you sold yourself short

You sold yourself

And blocked up your veins
With white powder dreams
Before the next time
We met.

And I loved till eternity
When the sun rose again
Our camper shelter
Toured us past endless love

And years later at a treatment centre
You met my sister and wrote me
You're a mother now
And I'm a father . . . of sorts

For a long time I tried halfhearted
Attempts to reach out to you
And you the same
Small efforts without reward

These days my heart warms
Now and then at the thought
Of you and I on the grass
Or in the woods

Fall 1984,
at Huupsitas,
for Michelle

Understanding Native Activism

STEVEN POINT

"The government and the natives, however, still are on a collision course because their objectives are mutually exclusive."

STEVEN POINT is a member of the Skowkale Band of the Sto:Lo Nation. A traditional spirit dancer whose Indian name means Mountain Stream, he is a well-regarded speaker on the topics of land claims and aboriginal rights. Prior to obtaining his law degree at the University of British Columbia, Steven worked as a land claims researcher, was chief of his band for seven years, and served on the executive committee of the Union of B.C. Indian Chiefs. At the University of British Columbia Steven's speciality was native land claims, and upon graduation he handled native rights cases for three years. He is currently working with Immigration Canada in the refugee adjudication directorate. Steven says his greatest accomplishment in life has been his successful marriage and the creation with his wife of their three children.

* * *

Why are more and more native peoples of Canada resorting to violence to achieve their political goals? Is it simply to raise the general public awareness of native concerns, or is it the beginning of a long-term commitment to the power of the gun as opposed to the power of the pen? It's my view that what begins as an awareness campaign can quickly evolve into an armed confrontation unless both sides have a clear communication channel open. When it comes to native issues, however, several barriers must be removed before this clear communication link can be established and maintained.

For too long there has been a general lack of understanding concerning native objectives and goals. This is true not only for government and the general public but also for the native peoples. In order for the process of communication to occur, the parties involved must be willing participants, open-minded and committed to solving the dilemma. Throughout the history of native/government relations these three elements were never present simultaneously. At times the government would be willing to negotiate, but the natives unable. At other times, the government was unwilling to participate — for example, when the Province of British Columbia would not enter negotiations with the Nisga'a.

Through the years the native strategies included petitions to the Queen of England, delegations to Ottawa and the United Nations, peaceful demonstrations, public awareness campaigns, and legal action. Through all of this the government's response was minimal, although there has been much rhetoric about the government's commitment to change. The government and the natives, however, still are on a collision course because their objectives are mutually exclusive. Native people want to remain distinct and be self-governing; government wants to end the Indian problem. To date, native land issues across Canada have been dealt with in different ways. Some tribes have entered into treaties with the federal government, whose constitutional responsibility it is to settle these matters. Other groups had not entered the process of treaty-making and still have not reached a common understanding as to aboriginal claims to land and resources.

In early times, the federal government met with native leaders, and after a relatively short time obtained free and clear title to vast tracts of land from the natives who gave up their land to the "whites forever." As time went on, natives began to realize how one-sided these treaties were. Natives were assigned to lands reserved for them, the title to which was held by the federal government. The natives received the use and benefit of these lands, but not title. The federal government assumed a parental role over natives, who, in the government's eyes, were unable to handle their own affairs. From the government's view that was correct. Native populations had been decimated by disease and poverty.

In British Columbia, like many other provinces, the responsibility to educate natives was dumped on the federal government. The natives were not wanted in the all-white public school system. Many church organizations, like the Catholic church, had for years been proselytizing among the native peoples. They began providing education services with the full financial support of the federal government. The physical and emotional abuse that happened to those natives who entered these residential schools is only now becoming public knowledge. Generally, the government proceeded on a clear policy of assimilating native people. Sometimes this occurred with native co-operation, but mostly it was an imposed policy.

Native people soon woke up from their fight with disease and alcoholism to find that their land and culture was dying out. The federal government helped this process along with its anti-potlatching laws that made it a criminal offence to sing and dance native songs and conduct the legal business traditionally done in the feast hall. Many native elders were arrested by Indian agents, then charged, convicted, and sentenced by the same agent for practising their spirituality. The native people also woke up to the fact that their fishing and hunting and trapping rights were being legislated out of existence. They saw their reserves shrinking beneath their feet due to highways and railways and power lines and gas lines. They woke up to the fact that even their own children were being taken away by over-zealous provincial social workers who lacked the cross-cultural awareness to appreciate the native way of life.

The unemployment rate on most reserves was well over 50 percent, and in many cases 100 percent of the population were on social assistance. Their homes were mostly substandard and overcrowded. Poverty and despair were the prelude to alcoholism and family abuse. All too often the letters from band councils to government authorities were never answered. The person on the street too often believed that natives got too much from government, that they paid no taxes and should be given no more rights and privileges than what other Canadians receive. It was easier to equate the drunken native on the street corner to all natives than to look beyond the facade and see the real situation. Native peoples began to agitate for better living conditions on their small reserves. They began holding demonstrations and sit-ins to raise public awareness.

Natives also began launching expensive legal cases like the *Calder* case, which went right to the Supreme Court of Canada. The aboriginal right to land then was viewed by the court as an usufructuary right — that is, a right to use of the land but not title. The right was described as "sui generis" — that is, a unique right, one not arising from known legal principles. The courts have been coming down with decisions that are viewed by natives as increasingly favourable, but recently a different view of aboriginal land rights has emerged. Originally there was a belief among natives that the courts had to be utilized. The federal government was not willing to negotiate on anything else but an extinguishment basis. The government required that to commence any negotiations over land claims, the Native Nations (as they began to be called) had to sign an agreement. They had to agree that at the end of negotiations they would extinguish their land/ claim to the land. Natives began to balk at such agreements. They began to demand a policy of non-extinguishment.

The natives wanted their claims recognized first and specific negotiations later. Leaders like the late George Manuel pressed for a continual recognition of aboriginal land claims through a process of native revenue-sharing to be paid to Indian government in perpetuity. Other leaders were of the "lock, stock and barrel" school. They wanted their land back plus compensation for lost resources to date; yet others began to agitate for complete sovereignty of their nations. Some even began issuing their own international passports. Amid all of this were cries from other groups like the Prairie Treaty Alliance who were pressing for the government to live up to the letter and intent of their old treaties, which by then had become constitutionally recognized and affirmed in section 35 of the Charter along with existing aboriginal rights.

Many other side issues also emerged. Environmentalists saw a way to get a broader base of support for their concerns by enlisting native groups. The traditionalists rejected this type of approach because it led to a protection of land and resources, not ownership and control. Those siding with environmentalists view the process as means to an end rather than the ultimate goal.

Another facet of native issues arose in Sechelt, British Columbia. The Sechelt band had negotiated an agreement that resulted, among other things, in the reserve land being turned over to the band. There was a general outcry in Indian country against this development because it was viewed by many as a sell-out. The provincial government was jubilant. The federal government announced with a fanfare that it had reached a historic plateau in government/native relations. The government for a long time had been pressing the natives towards a settlement of claims that would result in giving municipal status to Indian bands. Indian bands feared that they would be no longer a federal responsibility but would be transferred to provincial government jurisdiction. This smacked of the 1969 White Paper policy announced by the federal government under the Trudeau Liberals. That policy suggested that the Indian Act be terminated and all lands be given to the bands. If the end of special status and constitutional protection of native reserve lands was totally unacceptable to natives nation-wide in 1969, why did it become acceptable to the Sechelt band? The difference was that the government wrote a special federal Act of Parliament that dealt specifically with the Sechelt band. The result was that the federal government's constitutional responsibility was not disturbed.

So, what does all of this mean? It means that the process of settling long outstanding native land issues and social problems is not a simple task. The many players involved in their several evolving agendas makes the task something like catching fish with greased hands. The federal government wants to get out of the native business. Its long-term objective seems to be to:

1. settle all outstanding native land disputes;

2. transfer responsibility of servicing native bands to the provincial government and to the bands themselves.

The provincial governments seem reluctant to become involved until some basic matters are clarified:

1. Who pays for settling native claims?
2. Do natives want out of Canada, or are we talking about expanding the nation land base and giving them some kind of say in resource management and control?

The natives themselves have to clarify:

1. Who benefits from land claims? Registered Indians only, or all natives under some type of blood or culture formula?
2. Do they want sovereignty, or something less? If so, what land is involved?
3. What kind of resource management and control is required?
   a) Membership or Management Boards,
   b) Total control of some resources, not others.
   c) Special hunting, fishing and trapping rights.
4. What happens after an agreement is reached? What will be the role of federal and provincial governments?

It is a complex problem requiring co-ordination, co-operation and good will on the part of all parties involved, not to mention the dollars needed to cover the cost of the research discussions and negotiations. Who will provide this clarification? At one time it was a simple meeting between the federal government and the natives. Now the provinces are involved, and even private interest groups are demanding a seat at the negotiating table.

The courts have provided some very important guidance, but the general view is that the main load must be carried by the parties involved through negotiation. Many native groups, however, have little to no faith in the fair negotiation process, and those groups pressing for total sovereignty will not bring their claims to the courts because they believe that those courts don't have legal jurisdiction over another sovereign state. There are still other native groups who have yet to organize their political machinery.

Every year, more young native people become aware of their own history. They distrust the government and the courts and, in some cases, their own band councils. They want action and results, not promises. The long-time policy promoted by many native leaders of diplomatic activism is viewed by these activists as slow and counter-productive. Some even argue that their own leadership has been bought out by the establishment. They see the native leadership attending hundreds of meetings each year in posh hotels. These "meeting goers" were accused of doing little else for their own communities except sit in these meetings and raise their arms at appropriate times. Although this narrow view of native leadership is incorrect, the resulting "bad faith" has only contributed to an already tense situation. What is needed is a lengthy process whereby native leaders can first meet their own people and define their own goals and objectives before getting involved in the formal negotiations with other parties. Some native groups have already completed this task; most have not.

So, why do more and more native groups agitate with more and more militancy? It is because they are frustrated and tired of waiting for government and native leaders to finally come to some fair and equitable solutions to native problems and land concerns. Any democracy is only as good as its ability to deal fairly with its citizens. The law must not only be fair; it must also be seen to be fair. Once the general citizenship no longer respects the law, the country gradually sinks into lawlessness. The native peoples of Canada have had a long-outstanding legitimate grievance with government. Native/government relations can only improve if these grievances are dealt with equitably.

Is it asking too much for the federal and provincial governments to sit down with native peoples and correct what is obviously an injustice to them? I think it's not only required, but it's also absolutely necessary in order to avoid future violent eruptions.

Today In Class (Every Day)

Just so that you know
All you well fed politicians,
Here's something more to chew on.
Perhaps it won't fit into your
Too large, and always open,
Mouths.

Today in class,
In Sister Marie's class
I said, "I'd like to tear
Jean Chrétien's left arm off
And stuff it down his throat."
He's the minister of Indian Affairs.

Today, in class
I felt a horrible anger.
I felt a terrible rage.
I embraced new violence.
My heart pumped hate.
It pumps hate every day.

It feeds on frustration
Like countless other hearts.
And, our hearts pump hate
Every day,
Pump hate
Every day.

Canadians look to the South,
And point their blood soaked fingers
At a painful ignorance there.
They have a new vision,
And we're just their nightmare,
Every day.

No politician from our country
Represents our deepest true feelings.
Nor do they represent our struggle.
They are mostly messengers for masters in Ottawa.
Our hearts know hate,
Every day.

Spring 1970,
at the Institute
for Adult Studies,
Victoria

Life on the 18th Hole

by David Neel

Artist's Statement

DAVID NEEL

This print is intended to serve as a reminder of an event in Canadian history. It points to a time when Canada was put on the international stage in the stand-off in Oka, Quebec. This image is NOT intended to serve as inspiration for armed resistance. It is meant rather to help the viewer to recall and reflect on the events of the summer of 1990. It was inspired by Picasso's "Guernica," painted in reaction to the bombing of Guernica, Spain during the Spanish Civil War. I wanted to do a print using my influence as a native artist. The result draws upon my heritage as a hereditary Kwagiutl artist and my training as a professional photographer. A silk screen photo-montage using graphics, news photography, and created photography combine in a print which is contemporary in execution and traditional in foundation. The central image comes from a Canadian Press photograph that ran on the cover of the *Globe and Mail* newspaper. The choice and use of colour, bilateral symmetry in composition, eagle feather and circle of life motif are stylistic of traditional graphics.

The Mohawk warrior symbolizes an individual pushed to his limit and having the will to stand his ground. How many of us can say we would have the strength to stand for what we believe, at all costs? The struggle of the Mohawk people is symbolic of the struggle of all First Nations people. The "10 little policemen" is a play on the nursery rhyme "1 little, 2 little, 3 little Indians," allowing the viewer to see the ethnocentric and racist roots of this children's nursery rhyme. They symbolize the Canadian government's inaction in dealing with the issues leading up to the Oka crisis, and the following militarization. The Circle is the circle of life, the arrows the four directions, four being the number of balance and completeness. The red dots represent the blood of man, one for each race: the red, the yellow, the black, and the white man. Jointly these remind us of the common bond of all men. The barriers between men and between races are erected, not inherent. Clearly it is up to individuals, not governments, to dismantle these barricades and work together to the benefit of all.

Life on the 18th Hole

DAVID NEEL

"Systems, such as the education, political and judicial system are being made to work in our favour. There is much to overcome, but I see hope."

DAVID NEEL is from the Kwagiutl nation and inherited the name Tlat'lala'wis' from his father. David comes from a well-known family of totem pole carvers and makers of traditional Kwagiutl regalia, and this is the direction he has followed in his art work. As his ancestors did, he works mainly in wood, creating masks and regalia from Kwagiutl mythology and potlatch culture. David is also a well-recognized photographer specializing in photographing people, most often in black and white and usually combined with commentary from the subject.

*　　*　　*

Oka, who now does not know that word and the struggle for justice that took place? The words and images of the long summer have left an indelible impression on the minds of Canada and the world. Few events in recent history have been so divisive for the nation. For three months the stand-off between determined Mohawks and the Canadian government was in the headlines and the lead story on our television sets. It became a symbol and a rallying point for natives across Canada in their efforts to have long-standing issues brought to Canada's attention.

For non-natives, it was another episode in the government's mishandling of aboriginal affairs, leaving a black mark on our international image. For the federal government and the Department of Indian Affairs, it was an old wound proving itself not yet healed, a thorn in the side to be removed as quickly and quietly as possible. In British Columbia, the crisis had special significance because the majority of the province is not under any treaty obligations. Natives have long been pressing for negotiations and defending disputed territory.

So now that the long, hot summer is over and the dust has settled, where did the seeds of the dispute begin, and why was it to become a symbol of a bigger issue? Now that we have been left with this as part of our Canadian heritage, where do we go from here? The governments made claims that native issues are overdue for settlement and that both levels of government, as well as the Canadian people, are ready to act. Was this crisis rhetoric, or are we entering a new era of native/white relations?

The record of the Canadian government in following through on promises made to aboriginal citizens is not reassuring. The dispute has, however, left us with the hope that the sacrifices of the Mohawks will push forward the process of fair negotiations. Hope is the major thing to come out of the stand-off. As the aboriginal people of this country followed the events, we felt somehow stronger. As though the strength of these men and women was our strength. The opponent was unbeatable in numbers and resources, but there was hope. As we rallied, marched, organized, and blockaded we felt strong. Like this was a turning point in our history. We had regained the strength and gained the knowledge to help our Mohawk brothers and sisters and ourselves at the same time. Who could have known that the dispute would galvanize the many nations into a group working towards the same goal — a just and peaceful settlement in Oka, Quebec?

These were heady times. Fresh from Elijah Harper's victory over the Meech Lake accord, we could smell the winds of change. Our chiefs went east and met in an attempt to find a peaceful settlement. They marched, they met with the minister of the Department of Indian Affairs, and the dispute rolled on. We had peace camps of people from many races. Hundreds of American Indians came but were turned back at the Canadian border.

Oka became the common bond, a symbol of the struggle we all endure, that our parents and their parents endured. The Canadian public also became aware. Aware of the high price of "progress," aware that its government was not settling long-standing grievances with First Nations people. And we all stood by our televisions watching the latest developments. Nothing makes news like a man with a gun. The foreign news loved it — an American magazine referred to it as "Canada's civil war."

It seems so ironic that the dispute arose out of an expansion of a golf course. On one hand there is a group of people willing to take up arms and die to protect territory they feel is theirs, and on the other side an expansion of a recreational facility. This is indicative of the way both federal and provincial governments handle land issues: one interest group is told negotiations will be held while at the same time title or resource rights are given to another interest group. Both groups are thus pitted against one another, leaving the government standing on the side lines with the Canadian people the loser.

Take as an example the Tsitika watershed, currently the subject of a dispute between MacMillan Bloedel and the Musgamagw tribal council.

This land has been named as part of a comprehensive land claim; the government has stated a number of times that it is ready to negotiate; at the same time it has given MacMillan Bloedel the go-ahead. In these kinds of circumstances, mistrust is bound to arise. The government must realize that it is in the interest of all parties to settle issues like Oka and the Tsitika through a consistent approach for the benefit of all Canadians. Native people want the opportunity to contribute to and benefit from society, not be excluded from it. The Canadian public is becoming aware of this, yet the Canadian government continues to maintain a policy of exclusion.

Oka was not solely about a golf-course expansion; it was about government inaction in dealing with the concerns of the Mohawks. There is no reason why at this time in Canada's history we should still be fighting over territory. Land claims concern non-native Canadians as much as native: why haven't they been attended to? The feeling all too evident in the past — that if these problems were ignored they would somehow go away — is no longer justified. Statements made by B.C. Premier Vander Zalm, federal Minister of Indian Affairs Tom Siddon, and Canadian Prime Minister Brian Mulroney indicate that they too see this.

It is the sacrifices of the people who manned the barricades in Oka that have helped to push forward our cause and bring the message to Canada and the world. It is in no one's best interest that long-standing disputes like Oka be allowed to simmer until the boiling point. It is up to the governments to see that the needs of the municipality and the Mohawks are met. Simply standing by ready to clean up the mess is not enough. In a democracy the responsibilities lie on the shoulders of the citizens to make our needs known to the public sector and on the elected leaders to respond.

Making the government take action on the needs and wants of the people is not always easy, as any First Nations person can tell you. Since the time of contact every conceivable tactic within the law has been tried. Everything from petitions, public meetings, rallies, delegations to meet the Queen, and court cases, to the cross-country constitutional railway express has been used. Progress has been slow and costly, though we have had our victories. Most recently the Sparrow decision went our way, as did the defeat of the Meech Lake Accord, which would, once again, have left First Nations people out of the process.

In dealing with an unjust bureaucracy, native people are finding it necessary to resort to civil disobedience. The chief advantage of this is that it gives voice to those who have none. Who was aware of the plight of the Mohawk people before the guns were drawn and the press came running? The Canadian government and business interests such as those involved in developing the eighteenth hole in Oka have standard means and access to getting their message across. Oka is a rare opportunity for studying government public relations strategy during crisis and the role of disinformation. Much can be learned, and I hope we have learned much.

It is difficult to stand on the outside and pass judgement on the use of arms by the Mohawk people. For myself, I can say I do not condone the use of arms, though I can judge no man for defending the land of his ancestors. But why does "the battle of the pines" in Oka affect you and me? No one is taking our land? This is best answered by Jenny Jack, a Tlingit woman from British Columbia who was at the barricades: "If they're going to walk all over people here, they're going to walk all over people in British Columbia."

People did start to realize this, as was demonstrated by committed support from natives and non-natives all across the country. We realized that standing together we are strong, that unified we have a voice that can be heard. "This is finally waking up native people, we're finally starting to fight back," Jenny Jack says.

But there is another important message here that the public missed. When we talk about justice for natives, we are really saying justice for all people.

There is not a separate justice for the Jew, the Arab, the Hispanic, and the Native. If there is indeed "justice" in Canada there is justice for all races or justice for none. This raises another question. Why is there such an imbalance of aboriginal people in the penal system? There is no simple answer. Mr. Mulroney claims Canada has a fair justice system. History does not bear out his claim.

Nor does Mohawk Ronald Crosse's appearance in court, where his badly bruised and battered face told the story of a "rough time and abuse" while in the custody of the *Sûreté du Québec*. His lawyer made claims of physical abuse, but these went unheeded. If the justice system is to retain its integrity, it must not appear to be involved in violence against the powerless. Under Canadian law, a prisoner is a ward of the state and not subject to punishment until found guilty. This is not the first time the *Sûreté du Québec* has shown its true colours. In 1981, the *Sûreté* attacked unarmed Micmac women and children. One officer was seen kicking a three-year-old child, and another was heard yelling, "god damned savages." The most vivid example of *Sûreté* actions is their failure to stop the stoning of women and children as they left the Kanesatake reserve. Long will this leave a stain on Canada's human rights image in the international community.

The *Sûreté* was not alone in its disregard of the Canadian law. The military was also reportedly acting above the law at Oka, as if the Emergencies Act had been invoked. According to University of Ottawa law professor Bradford Moses, "it seems the military is very clearly acting in violation of its own authority. It's completely unregulated." The army also violated the human rights of the Mohawk people. As André Paradis of the Quebec Civil Liberties Union put it, "the actions of the army are in violation of constitutional rights." This did not go unnoticed internationally: Archbishop Desmond Tutu spoke out publicly against the handling of Oka, as did American black activist Jesse Jackson, who also visited Kanesatake but was not permitted to visit the Warriors. Even the Pope questioned Prime Minister Mulroney about human rights violations at Oka. Canada has simultaneously lost its naivety about the concerns of its first citizens and sustained damage to its image as a supporter of human rights.

To better understand the Mohawk stand-off at Oka, it is necessary to know a little of the history of the Six Nations Confederacy and its relationship with Canada. In 1664, the Six Nations Confederacy signed a treaty expressly detailing its sovereignty. The Six Nations were British allies against the French, and later the Americans. They were not subjects of the Crown: they were referred to as "His Majesty's allies," and their lands were theirs to "enjoy forever," under the King's "protection." This promising beginning was not maintained. By the early nineteenth century native Indians had become subordinate, and the federal Indian Act of 1876 continued the encroachment and bureaucratic control over their lives.

In 1890 a petition by the hereditary chiefs demanded recognition of their autonomy and their exemption from the Act. At this time a longstanding system of hereditary chiefs was in place, and there were reformers interested in replacing this system with an elected system. The reformers got their way. An 1890 amendment to the Indian Act permitted the Department of Indian Affairs to install this system without band consent. In 1894, 212 Six Nations men sent a petition to Ottawa demanding an elective council. Opponents of the hereditary system were known as the Dehorners, Six Nations Rights Association, Indian Rights Association, or the Warriors Association.

The days of the hereditary system finally drew to a close with the appointment of Colonel C. E. Morgan as Indian superintendent at Brantford in 1923. He was a veteran of the Boer War and had worked as a colonial administrator in South Africa. His was a policy of firm action and constant police vigilance. On October 7, 1924, Colonel Morgan, along with a number of armed Mounties, arrived at a council meeting with an order-in-council abolishing the ancient hereditary system. An election was called, in which only 16 to 30 percent of the eligible voters participated, resulting in a primarily Christian band council. Under the elected system Six Nations autonomy continued to dwindle and bureaucratic control increased. Ongoing attempts at regaining control were undertaken by the chiefs. These included petitions, legal actions, and trips to London and Geneva.

The Canadian government continues to deny the sovereignty and right to self-government of native peoples, despite the requirements placed on it by its own laws. The Canadian Constitution, section 35(1), recognizes and affirms "existing aboriginal and treaty rights of the aboriginal peoples of Canada." But it is only through the long and costly system of the courts that exactly what this means is being defined, as in the Sparrow case. Further, the Canadian government assumes a "fiduciary responsibility" under the Indian Act in which it purports to uphold and look out for the rights of first citizens. By attempting to override native self-government, the provincial and federal governments have exceeded their own constitutional jurisdiction. It can be argued that at Oka the Mohawks were defending legitimate constitutional jurisdiction and that the government has been illegally enforcing usurpation of that jurisdiction.

The situation of the Six Nations is not unlike that of British Columbia's native people in that they too have never surrendered their land and sovereignty. By Canada's own laws and by international law a sovereign association exists. Here again, the common ground occupied by British Columbians and those involved in the situation at Oka becomes apparent. As we watch the court battle unravel, we should see legal argument brought out that pertains to the land/sovereignty question across Canada.

So where do we go from here? We have seen a perhaps unprecedented galvanizing of natives from across the country. One woman commented to me recently that she wished we could retain that feeling, that momentum. Perhaps we can. We have seen Six Nations men and women risk their lives and the security of their future for something they believe in. This is something I was brought up to value and admire. We have witnessed a time of crisis, the government inaction that led up to it, and the military aftermath. We are about to witness a legal extravaganza as the battle is brought into the courtroom. Canada is perhaps not as close-lipped, blind, and deaf to native concerns as it was. We have seen that government handling of First Nations issues has not progressed.

On one hand government will promise the world and with the other it will "expropriate" your land. Since the surrender of Kanesatake there have been two orders-in-council expropriating native reserve land in British Columbia — one involving the Mount Currie Indian Band, and the other the Boothroyd Indian band. This from a government promising to put native land claims as first priority. It is interesting to note that when the government takes land from natives it is "expropriation," and when the natives resist it is "militancy." One thing we can learn from Oka is that the government will do as it pleases. It is only by bringing public attention to Canada and what is happening here that we will focus attention on our needs. We must take our message beyond the borders of Canada and seek support internationally. The African National Congress, so widely recognized and supported, has over thirty offices worldwide.

Oka was about justice. Native sovereignty and self-determination are about justice. We are at a point in Canadian history where it is no longer as easy for government bureaucrats to suppress the needs of the first citizens. As stated by columnist Stephen Hume,

This, the first generation since Louis Riel to dare to dream big dreams, was nurtured by powerful born-again cultural pride. Its young people transcend a century's attempts at assimilation. They are the best educated youth in Canadian history; they have computers and cellular phones. Tiny isolated reserves are integrated into national political awareness.

As I sit working at my computer, I like to think that we are learning, that the sacrifices made at Oka will not be wasted, that my children will be living in a more just Canada. Education is changing the way native people relate to the larger society. Elders from across this province have told me education is the key. Systems such as the educational, political, and judicial system are being made to work in our favour. There is much to overcome, but I see hope.

A passage from the Two Row Wampum Treaty of the Six Nations reads:

These two rows will symbolize two paths or two vessels, travelling down the same rivers together. One, a birch bark canoe, will be for the Indian people, their laws, their customs and their ways. The other, a ship, will be for the white people and their laws, their customs and ways. We shall each travel the river together, side by side, but in our own boat. Neither of us will try to steer the other's boat.

In Canada we have seen a rocking of these boats.

SOURCES

Clark, Bruce. Indian Heroes, Government Outlaws. *Globe and Mail*, 26 September 1990.

Hume, Stephen. Black Eye for a Mohawk Is a Black Mark for Justice. *Vancouver Sun*, 3 October 1990.

———— It's Time to Reshape a Shattered Illusion. *Vancouver Sun,* 31 August 1990.

———— We Will Never Know Innocence Again. *Vancouver Sun,* 21 September, 1990.

Mathew, Keith. Koyote Tales. Kahtou. November 1990.

O'Neil, Peter. Woman Defied Armed Might. *Vancouver Sun,* 4 September 1990.

Ottawa Citizen. Army Claimed Acting Above Law in Oka Row. *Vancouver Sun,* 20 September 1990.

Ripstein, Arthur. The Use of Violence Advances No Cause. *Globe and Mail,* 11 September 1990.

Titley, Brian. A Narrow Vision. Duncan Campbell Scott and the Administration of Indian Affairs in Canada. University of British Columbia Press, 1986. Vancouver, B.C.

Wright, Ronald. Does Canada Want a Wounded Knee? *Globe and Mail,* 30 August 1990.

Three Musts

The Yakwiimit did it,
Perhaps even as a lifestyle.
The ones that made first contact did it;
We are the living proof of that.
Each generation that followed
Did the same;
They all survived.
We must struggle to survive.
Our life? . . . a struggle for survival.

We need to protect our lives.
We must protect our children.
We have to protect our communities.
We have so much to protect.

Sobriety is a development,
Learning is a development,
Solidarity is a development,
Protest is a development,
Awareness is a development,
Discussion is a development
Our lives must be development.

circa 1968-75,
in Victoria

The Value of First Nations Languages

PATRICK KELLY

"One of the strongest gains to be realized by Canada and British Columbia in encouraging First Nations educational ideas to flourish is that the creative energy of the First Nations people, so long suppressed by social, economic, and political barriers would be made available for everyone's benefit."

PATRICK KELLY is a member of the Lakahahmen band of the Sto:lo nation. He was born in Mission, British Columbia in September 1952. Patrick studied education at the University of British Columbia and worked as a support worker to native students for many years. He currently holds the position of Senior Officer of Native Programs for the B.C./Yukon Region of the Department of the Secretary of State for Canada, where for several years he has been involved in the development of policies and programs to promote the retention of native languages. He is the father of five children.

* * *

A Whole-Life Context

Communication is essential in a world where change is the standard. Interpersonal communication messages, for both sender and receiver, are influenced by cultural and knowledge reference points that exist within every person. The heritage of First Nations people is popularly promoted and understood to include traditions, values, and beliefs that holistically link the people interdependently to the world around them. That assumption is important to understand the nature of the message here. First Nations languages are important unto themselves but are best considered in a whole-life context.

A Multi-dimensional Problem

Language is an important vehicle for cultural expression, for it is largely through language that unique cultural experience is shared. It is well known that some concepts do not translate easily from one language to another. For example, a provincial court judge recently intimated to a tribal leader (they had been working closely together on common justice problems for almost two years) that he was troubled by a difficult problem in which some of the judge's peers could not see how the courts could adopt some of the tribe's traditional justice methods of dealing with tribal members convicted by the courts. The judge worried that the differences between the tribal and court methods were irreconcilable and that the attitudes of his peers would anger the First Nations people so much that they would not want to work further with the courts. The tribal leader was puzzled by the judge's concern, for he thought they had been working well together. The tribal leader realized he and his people were working according to their traditions but had not told the judge explicitly what those were. He explained that the solution to the judge's problem was q'eq'otel (pronounced Kwa-kwel-tel from Halq'emeylem [pronounced Hal-kem-ay-lem] — a Salish language) meaning "to meet." The judge was puzzled because he thought they had been doing that already. One word seemed such a simplistic solution, but the Halq'emeylem term actually linked the judges into the tribe's traditional governing process in which q'eq'otel is a first step. The solution resulted in a meeting between the judges and the First Nations community leaders in which they worked out their problem.

The foregoing example illustrates the multi-dimensional nature of language problems. One word or simple phrase in one language can actually mean a complex process in another. Attitudes and community relations are invariably part of language problems. The cultural context of one language may not be easily understood when seen or heard from the perspective of another culture using a different language. Governing principles and philosophical approaches may be different. The challenge of working with language problems is multi-faceted.

A Diverse Cultural Base

Sixty-three percent or seven of the eleven First Nations language families (defined in volume I, *Historical Atlas of Canada*, as "related languages of common origin," Plate 66, 1987) that exist in Canada exist in British Columbia. They are Athapaskan, Tlingit, Haida, Tsimshian, Wakashan, Salish, and Kootenay. The latter six exist solely in British Columbia. It is clear that First Nations make up a rich cultural resource in British Columbia.

Pressures Against Survival

No one likes the feeling or to admit that part of their heritage and identity is dying or lost. The very nature of this subject is troublesome. For many First Nations people, succumbing to this would be admitting that the early attempts at their assimilation through government and church efforts have succeeded. Nevertheless, recent studies show that some First Nations languages are critically close to being lost forever.

The Assembly of First Nations September 1990 report "Towards Linguistic Justice For First Nations" finds that 66 percent of First Nations languages across Canada are declining, endangered, or critical (based on a survey of 151 bands). Fifteen percent are flourishing, and the remainder are enduring.

A January 1988 report entitled "Critical Conditions of Traditional Languages in British Columbia," prepared by Bill Mussell for the Department of the Secretary of State, concluded that "traditional (indigenous) languages spoken by the status Indian peoples of British Columbia are in serious condition and require substantial support for their survival. People over the age of 40 represent the main population of speakers of all but a few of the languages." Mussell further reports of the Salish group that "their combined population is about 26,500. Only 3,000 of these people can speak their traditional language." With only 11 percent of the Salish population able to speak their traditional language, the pressures against their language surviving, considering numbers alone, are immense. Add to that the events of everyday living (school, business, community living, etc.) occurring in the official languages of Canada (mostly English in British Columbia), and it becomes clear that unless drastic efforts are made to retain and revitalize most First Nations languages in British Columbia, their only legacy will be found in archives.

Assisting Survival

A comparison of how languages are treated in Canada will help to clarify possible future actions needed for the survival of First Nations languages. The official languages of Canada (English and French) are protected under federal law by statute, including the Charter of Rights and Freedoms, and by policy and programs ($372.6 million for French in 1988-89). The languages of Canada's multicultural communities (commonly known as "Heritage Languages") are supported under federal programs of the Ministry of State for Multiculturalism ($3.7 million in 1988-89) and Canada Employment and Immigration. Federal legislation has been proposed to create a department for multiculturalism, which suggests that heritage languages would gain new impetus in federal government support. Currently, the status of most First Nations languages in federal schemes is at the program stage ($1 million in 1988-89, Secretary of State) with the exception of those in the Yukon and Northwest Territories, where five-year federal-territorial agreements are in place totalling $21 million combined from 1985 to 1990.

The British Columbia government in May 1990 announced a "five-year, $10.7 million initiative to help preserve and strengthen the culture and language of British Columbia's Native Peoples." Native heritage, language, and culture centres would be developed in British Columbia with the program under the direction of a Native Advisory Committee representing all the major tribal groups in the province. The program remains in its early stages of development, and it is too early to assess its success.

The Assembly of First Nations (AFN) has recommended that "First Nations language and culture must receive equivalent recognition, protection and promotion in the Canadian constitution, and through enabling legislation, as that of official languages" (*Towards Linguistic Justice for First Nations*, 1990). Whereas the government response to the AFN is not yet known, future federal support cannot be ascertained. The AFN argues "that the Government of Canada has a moral obligation to rectify previous government action to suppress our (First Nations) language and culture."

Motivation to Succeed

First Nations language survival efforts must be directed at the learner, for without people speaking them, the languages cannot survive. This seems like a trite comment, but not when it comes to choosing priorities for limited funds and other resources. There are many competing demands for language-program activity ranging from linguistic research, pedagogical research and curriculum development, language policy research and development, teacher training, conferences, and many others. Certainly all are needed. However, unless all such activities are directed at assisting learners, their value is severely limited. All efforts must eventually end up assisting to motivate the language learner.

As stated at the outset, the whole-life context is important to the teaching traditions of First Nations. Traditional education methods usually revolved around elders. Minnie Peters of the Sto:lo Nation has said, "Our Elders speak from the heart of this Land." Chief Seattle said, "Teach your children what we have taught our children — that the earth is our mother." Cheryl Arnouse and Lori Jules of the Shuswap nation have said, "Our language is what separates us from other people of the world; with our language, we are unique and rich in culture." The preceding quotations encompass more than language, but especially they reflect the holistic values that underlie traditional First Nations culture and language. Consequently, the challenge of motivating First Nations language learners is complex if full traditional value is to be imparted.

Value is the key. If First Nations language and culture can be restored as honourable qualities in a person's education, only then will a person want to gain such qualities. Otherwise, the learner will focus on other knowledge that is considered valuable. School curriculum reflects what a society values. First Nations language and culture do not form an integral part of the British Columbia school core curriculum. They should.

The value of First Nations language and culture in school curriculum should be recognized to help reduce perceived systemic discrimination against the heritage of the First Nations learner. An invisible barrier exists and works against motivation except in schools where First Nations languages are taught or those run by native people themselves in which there is usually culturally relevant curriculum.

The bottom line expected of education today usually focuses on job skills. However, if the generally problematic condition of much of the environment, of the job market and of society today is an indication of the success of this approach to education, it may be time to include aspects of the holistic approaches promoted by First Nations. Business cannot be separated from the environment. The environment cannot be separated from government. Government cannot be separated from social and economic issues. People cannot be separated from all of the above. Perhaps it is time to recognize this and make efforts to reinstate a whole-life perspective in education. Teaching First Nations languages would contribute to understanding such concepts given that such holistic or whole-life values are embedded in them.

Remove the Barriers

Arrangements between federal, provincial, local, and First Nations governments are needed to accommodate the teaching of First Nations languages. If it is accepted by all parties that culture is becoming increasingly important to people throughout the world today, it should not be too difficult to make adequate arrangements for good culturally relevant education. Rather than look for jurisdictional barriers to stifle such development, all parties must make a good effort to work together. All parties would stand to gain from mutually developed plans.

One of the strongest gains to be realized by Canada and British Columbia in encouraging First Nations educational ideas to flourish is that the creative energy of First Nations people, so long suppressed by social, economic, and political barriers, would be made available for everyone's benefit. Recent economic development positions expressed by First Nations governments include concepts that focus on renewable resource development, sustainable economic development, environmentally sensitive development, community control of decision-making, and ideas reflecting similar themes. There are words for such ideas in First Nations languages. There are also words that explain how such concepts work. Surely Canadians can support barriers being removed that would permit First Nations people to re-assert their holistic concepts of the world. True integration in Canadian society would permit First Nations citizens to contribute values and ideas equally alongside those of other Canadians.

Prospects for the Future

Among the many recommendations proposed in the Mussell and Assembly of First Nations reports, the following seem to capture the essence of immediate and short-term needs:

- Native people must recognize that the language belongs to them, that it is their responsibility, and that only THEIR efforts will keep it alive. (Mussell)

- First Nations language and culture must receive recognition, protection, and promotion in the Canadian constitution, and through enabling legislation, equivalent to that given the official languages. (AFN)

- Elder speakers' knowledge or cultural traditions, language skills, fluency, and ways of presentation, such as body language, should be collected, recorded, and documented. Such information should be filmed/recorded by native people with the assistance of competent technicians who are willing to share their expertise. (Mussell)

- Day care and preschools that will provide immersion or bilingual language instruction must be promoted. (AFN)

- Time should be allocated at specific meetings for the expression of problems and for seeking ways in which to resolve issues. A tenet of these group-solving processes should be the bringing together of people rather than the taking of divisive positions. (Mussell) Though proposed for First Nations language groups, this method could apply equally to cross-cultural sharing between First Nations people and other Canadians.

- An Aboriginal Languages Foundation should be established immediately
to carry out such activities necessary to ensure the perpetuation, revitalization, growth, and protection of First Nations languages. (AFN) Verna
Kirkness, Director of the First Nations House of Learning at the University of British Columbia, in a report that she prepared in 1988 for the
Department of the Secretary of State for Canada, has already recommended the formation of a national First Nations Language Foundation.
And Bill C-269, presented to the federal Parliament in November 1989
by Member of Parliament Ethel Blondin, proposed "An Act to establish
the Aboriginal Languages Foundation." No action has, however, yet
been taken, and it remains an unresolved issue.

The provincial Native Advisory Committee on Heritage, Language and
Culture, in its July 1989 report, proposed several recommendations. As
noted earlier, the provincial government announced its response to the
report in May 1990. One recommendation that propels language initiatives
beyond the usual social policy boundaries states:

The Ministry of Native Affairs should be charged with proactively integrating
this initiative with Native participants, key provincial ministries, inter-ministry
committees, central agencies, local municipalities, regional governments, and
educational institutions.

The committee's explanation of possible economic benefits positioned the
language and culture initiative as part of British Columbia's growing tourism industry in which First Nations cultural centres would enhance the
province's reputation as a desirable destination for Canadian and international travellers. In explaining further the benefits of its proposal, the
committee stated,

The cultural benefits, which will accrue to Native and non-Native British
Columbians alike, include a better understanding and celebration of the differences between native and non-native cultures. This has obvious implications
for improved relations between the native community and the larger community in all aspects of daily life in British Columbia.

The cross-cultural education and economic dimensions of language and
culture programs provide enhanced prospects for First Nations and other
citizens to work constructively together.

There seems to be a changing atmosphere across Canada in which
governments at all levels are being encouraged to address pressing First
Nations issues. Among the most subtle and potentially most valuable is
language. Let us hope that the efforts by the provincial government and
further considerations by the federal government will enable First Nations

people to contribute their share of shaping how the world of the future develops. If the proper value of whole-life education can be realized, Canada and British Columbia would be better for that. The provincial court judge and the tribal leader realized, when dealing together on common issues, that it was possible to reach workable solutions that respected both cultures. Understanding one First Nations word made the difference. Imagine the value of all British Columbia First Nations languages. If they are lost, they cannot be recovered, because British Columbia is the only part of the world where they exist.

My Blanket, My Story

I want you to make a book about
My blanket.
It seems such a shame all that work.

That blanket just sits in my home;
More people should see it,
And know how it got made.
More people could share it.

I just can't seem to write,
I try, but it doesn't work very well.
The words just don't come,
The words just don't.

I think it could be good,
My work, my blanket, my story.
Such a shame,
People could share it.

Spring 1990,
at Musqueam

The Children of Tomorrow's Great Potlatch

ERNIE CREY

"The day will soon come when First Nations people and whites will sit together to take part in the greatest potlatch of all. They will talk and sing about the wonderful world they will be leaving for their children."

ERNIE CREY is a member of the Cheam band of the Sto:lo nation. He has been active in the native community in a professional capacity since 1970. As a Community Development Officer, he has worked in remote communities across the province. As a professionally trained social worker, Ernie pioneered the province's first Aboriginal Child Welfare program with the Union of B.C. Indian Chiefs in 1975. Late in the 1970s he joined the public service of Canada, first as a Recruitment Officer and Senior Management Staffing Officer with the Public Service Commission, and later as an Economic Development Officer with the Department of Fisheries and Oceans. Ernie was elected Provincial Vice-President of the United Native Nations in 1988 and continues to serve in that capacity.

* * *

We dream of the day when First Nations people and whites will sit together to take part in a great potlatch. Before this happens, the whites must learn more of the First Nations history, because understanding is essential to create solutions and harmony.

The Indian Act of 1876 shattered the lives of the aboriginal people of Canada. It imprisoned Canada's aboriginal people on tracts of land called reserves and in tandem with both colonial and provincial legislation permitted any non-Indian male over the age of eighteen to simply occupy up to three hundred and twenty acres of the aboriginal peoples' tribal homelands. In British Columbia, the colonial Governor James Douglas encouraged the notion that the Indians ought to pre-empt land after the fashion of whites but this policy was soon reversed by Sir Joseph Trutch. He was a surveyor who was to become the chief architect of Indian policy in British Columbia after Douglas's retirement in 1864. In addition to the loss of tribal homelands through the process of pre-emption, the Indian Act outlawed all aboriginal religious ceremonies and practices from 1880 to 1951. This legislation also made it impossible for aboriginal people to take part in the political and economic life of the industrial society springing up just outside the bounds of the reserves. As residents of B.C., Indians were denied the provincial vote and the opportunity to hold public office in the provincial government until 1949. In Canada, all Indians were denied the right to vote in federal elections and the opportunity to hold federal public office until 1960. This meant that Indians had no voice in shaping either legislation or policies affecting their lives for nearly a century. All decisions affecting Indians were to be the private preserve of White politicians in Victoria or in Ottawa until more than halfway through the next century. So all-pervasive was the Indian Act in the lives of Indian people in B.C., that Native people or lawyers acting on their behalf could be jailed without recourse of law for advocating Indian land rights in the period from 1927 to 1951. As absurd as it was, Indian agents also roamed British Columbia Indian reserves to make sure the houses were kept tidy.   (Mathias, 1986:2)

While it is easy to identify the wrongs of this legislation and the damaging impact it had on all native peoples, those most profoundly damaged were the children of the First Nations peoples.

Residential Schools

Dr. Neil MacDonald of the University of Manitoba has described in an interview (24 May 1989) the practice of "Fall round-up" in which the children of the First Nations peoples were gathered in groups or "rounded up" to be taken to the residential schools:

It is near the turn of the century. Indian agents, RCMP constables, and non-Native farmhands encircle a Manitoba Indian reserve. One of the Indian agents and an RCMP constable approach the house of an Indian family, bang on the door and loudly demand the parents give up their children to them. The parents have barricaded the door and refuse to answer. The Indian agent instructs the RCMP constable to break down the door. They rush into the house, pry the frightened, screaming children from their parents' arms and rush them to a holding area outside. The constable and agent go to the next house and the next and in the ensuing few days this scene is repeated many times on this reserve and on most reserves in Southern Manitoba. All children captured during "Fall round-up" are marched to the nearest CPR station, assigned a number and unceremoniously herded into cattle cars for transport to the residential school at Winnipeg.

Dr. MacDonald described another incident as told to him by an Indian agent who took part in "Fall round-up":

The Indian agent was sitting on his horse after his group of children had been loaded onto the train and noticed a dust cloud in the distance. Thinking it was more agents bringing their shipment of children he called for the train to wait for the new arrivals. When the group of people arrived at the station, he found they were not the agents and children but the mothers of the children he had rounded-up. The women ran alongside the cattle cars until they found their child or children. They grabbed the hands of their children and refused to let go, thus preventing the train's departure. The RCMP constables responded by climbing up the sides of the cars and stomped on the hands of the mothers, breaking their grips and some of their hands and fingers. The train then departed for Winnipeg.

Abhorrent scenes such as those described above occurred in many parts of Canada in this past century. Margaret George of the Sto:lo nation of the Fraser Valley in British Columbia, and now a member of the Burrard band, confirms that First Nations children of British Columbia underwent similar experiences. She remembers (5 October 1990) that upon being removed from her home as a child she was taken to a cattle pen at Agassiz, where she was assigned a number and measured for her height. The children were not trusted to know how old they were and so were sent to various residential schools across the province according to their height rather than their actual age. She states that siblings were frequently sent to separate schools, but in instances of being at the same institution were not permitted contact with each other. The children were removed at age five and remained in the residential schools until age sixteen. Contact with parents was strongly discouraged and strictly limited. A number of children returned to their homes during summer months but were estranged from their families because they no longer spoke or understood their native tongue. They also had a new set of behaviours and values their families could not understand. Those children who remained at the schools throughout the summer months had no contact with family or community members for the many years they were confined to the schools.

First Nations children in British Columbia were compelled by the Indian Act to attend the residential schools. The first of these schools appeared in British Columbia in the 1880s and continued to operate until the latter 1960s. Thus, four generations of aboriginal children were raised during their most formative years outside the influence of their home communities. As Randy Fred points out in his Introduction to Celia Haig-Brown's *Resistance and Renewal: Surviving the Indian Residential School,* the bridge between generations which would have permitted the transfer of cultural knowledge from one generation to the next had been virtually destroyed. (Haig-Brown, 1988:12)

In the residential schools powerful measures were taken by the caretakers of the children to force the children to abandon their languages and dissuade them from identifying with the lifestyle and values of their parents. Those who attended the schools recall horrific tortures and beatings at the hands of their care-takers for speaking their native language. (Comeau and Stantin, 1990:96)

A Salish elder, Henry Castle, recalled (interview, September 11, 1990) the punishment he received for speaking Halkomelem, the language of the Coast Salish people:

When his classmates were caught speaking their language one day at Coqualeetza school near Chilliwack they had their mouths pried open and sewing needles driven through their tongues into the bottom of their mouths by their caretakers. This type of treatment is corroborated in contemporary literature. (Haig-Brown 1988:11)

Recent reports dealing with the residential schools focus on the horrendous physical and sexual abuse many native children suffered while in these institutions. Abuse of this nature follows its victims throughout their lives and colours their relationships with others. Those who have written about these institutions emphasize those aspects of the institutions designed to assimilate aboriginal children. Undoubtedly, the religious denominations operating these schools under contract with the federal government wanted the children to embrace their particular brand of Christianity. (Tennant, 1990:79) However, the federal government and private wealth in British Columbia were strongly motivated and committed to the establishment of these institutions for their own reasons.

So it was that, coincident with the creation of the residential schools, the Indian Act was amended to outlaw potlatches. (Tennant, 1990:51) The potlatches were outlawed not exclusively at the behest of the Christian denominations active in missionary work in that era — government officials and individuals at the head of fishing and lumber companies also wanted the "potlatch laws" introduced. In this case, however, it was not because they cared whether potlatches were "heathen" practices or not but because potlatches took Indian people from village to village, thereby depriving those companies of the Indian labour they were determined to have. (Glavin, 1990:82). To the federal government and resource companies, the residential schools represented a workforce the companies could draw on in future in order to expand their wealth and thereby their influence on the Pacific coast. However, as European immigration increased, interest in Indian labour subsided. White hands replaced brown hands on the cannery lines, in the sawmills, and out on the fishing grounds.

To the Christian denominations, the residential schools were factories producing souls for Christ. To the Indians, however, the schools came to represent the loss of their children. Parents and children were made strangers to each other. In the schools, children did not learn the meaning of family — what it meant to be son or daughter, brother of sister, aunt or uncle. Therefore, when many of the children who had survived the residential school experience returned home and started their own families, they found themselves ill-prepared to be parents. It is a universal truth that one learns to be a parent in a family, not in an institutional setting. (Miller, 1989: 196). The social order in aboriginal communities is built on the extended family. The schools virtually obliterated Indian family life and, therefore, severely compromised the social order of most Indian communities. In part, this is what is at the base of many of the social ills in Indian communities. Infant mortality rates are three times greater for native infants than for non-native. Three times more native children than non-native children will take their own lives. Ninety-five percent of all native children enrolled in schools will drop out by grade 12. The high incidence of family violence and poor health due to diseases linked to self-destructive lifestyles and poverty continue to tear at the fabric of First Nations families. (Comeau and Stantin, 1990: 79). These grim statistics are, in part, the continuing legacy of the residential schools. Unfortunately for Indians, residential schools were to remain a fixture in British Columbia until the 1960s. It is a grim irony that throughout the entire era of the residential schools, white people and their churches would loudly extol the virtues of family life.

After the Second World War, the economy of British Columbia expanded at a rate unprecedented in its history. The coffers of the provincial government swelled in large measure due to the rate at which its resource-rich land mass was being exploited. Ottawa and Victoria would now introduce a wide range of social programs and educational opportunities for its citizens. Sadly, in this same era the aboriginal people of B.C. were all but forgotten. First Nations families had been relegated to a gray world on reserves and would not join in the "great potlatch" being given by the governments.

Child Welfare

In the late 1960s, rows of small, dark children were marched from the remaining residential schools in the province. As the children were led to the waiting buses to be taken to the planes and trains which would take them back to their home communities, the keys were turned in the locks of the great doors, forever closing the residential schools and marking the end of an era.

Now that the schools were closed, bureaucrats met in air-conditioned offices in Victoria and Ottawa trying to decide which senior level of government would take on the responsibility for the protection and care of Indian children. Outside consultants were canvassed for their views and recommendations on how best to extend child welfare to Indian children. H. B. Hawthorne, the author of a study entitled "A Survey of the Contemporary Indians of Canada: A Report on Economic, Political, Educational Needs and Policies," wrote about the jurisdictional confusion over the responsibility of child welfare services on reserve. He described child welfare services to Indians in most of Canada as being unsatisfactory to appalling. Hawthorne recommended that child welfare services of each province be extended to the reserves and that the Indians be induced to accept this arrangement. However, no thought was given as to whether or not these services were compatible with the needs or wishes of the Indian communities.

Much of the wrangling between Ottawa and Victoria over child welfare services to Indians was rooted in differences over which government would pay for these services. Both the provinces and the federal government remain uncertain as to who is really responsible for child welfare on reserve. For now, Victoria is happy to apprehend Indian children on reserve, leaving Ottawa to pick up the bill while the children are in care.

Like the dark-frocked missionaries of old who were determined to save native children from satanic forces, the bureaucrats in their dark three-piece suits set out to rescue native children from the new devils of post World War II Canada, namely poverty, "unsanitary" homes, and neglectful parents. No turn-of-the-century missionary pursued his work among the Indians with greater vigour than the freshly scrubbed young social workers assigned to inquire into the welfare of Indian children newly returned from the residential schools. These graduates of reputable schools of social work had learned their lessons well. An elderly couple on a reserve was an inappropriate resource for a child whose parents were away working in a cannery or perhaps out on a trapline or tending fishing nets on either the Skeena or Fraser Rivers. Multi-generational households were not good for children either, and therefore a child's presence in one was good cause to remove him or her. Any dwelling which lacked the amenities of a suburban community also prompted the social workers to remove children. Evidence of alcohol consumption in an Indian home was sufficient reason to take a child. Reports of neglect from reliable informants like school teachers, priests, or Indian agents needed no investigation and therefore were good enough reason to apprehend children. After a while, local white merchants, commercial fishermen, and taxi-cab drivers came to be regarded, in the eyes of the social workers, as reliable witnesses to the failings of Indian parents.

In 1955, of the 3,433 children placed in protective care in British Columbia, less than 1 percent (twenty-nine) were native. By 1964, native children represented 34.2 percent (1,446) of the total 4,228 children in care. According to Patrick Johnston, author of "Native Children and the Child Welfare System," native children accounted for 36.7 percent of all children in care in British Columbia in 1980, even though only 3.5 percent of all children in the province were native. According to Johnston, the placement of non-native children was usually a temporary situation. This was not so for native children who were either shuffled from one foster home to another for years or adopted, mostly by non-native families. The majority never returned home.

In the early 1960s and 1970s many Indian children adopted by whites were removed by their new families to countries overseas or to locations in the United States. Many adoptions of Canadian Indian children were arranged by social workers who did not give a second thought to the implications of sending thousands of aboriginal children to other countries. The patronizing logic of the early missionaries and decision-makers in Ottawa was reflected in the decisions of these new "protectors" of the Indian children.

While the conditions under which the children lived in the church-run schools of a decade earlier were deplorable, at least the parents of the children knew where they were. Children taken into care by the provincial Child Welfare authorities could be anywhere in the province. In the case of adoption, members of a child's family or band council knew it was just as possible for the child to be in Australia as in Canada. What is more, the children were now to experience a sense of isolation greater than that which they had experienced in the church-run schools. In the schools, the children may have been occasionally visited by a relative or a friend of the family, or they may have breached the rules to socialize with a sibling. The foster home system often did not hold out this opportunity. In the case of adoption the child would, in most cases, never be seen or heard of again by his or her family.

The apprehension of First Nations children continues to this day. Half the population of First Nations people now live off reserve, and, accordingly, one half or more of recent apprehensions of native children take place in urban settings. This gives the lie to the claim of provincial Child Welfare authorities that apprehensions of Indian children are on the decline in British Columbia. The urban ghetto is now the environment from which Indian children must be rescued.

Leaders of First Nations communities and organizations in British Columbia continue their struggle to resolve the "land title" question and have aboriginal rights enshrined in Canada's constitution, while faceless bureaucrats in both Victoria and Ottawa continue their low-profile debate over who is responsible for Child Welfare programs and their costs. As for children in need of protection, major newspapers in British Columbia still report cases of social workers ushering Indian children into flea-bag motels under the care of unskilled child-care workers because of the lack of adequate foster homes.

Publicly overshadowed by the larger legal and political fights between First Nations and the federal and provincial governments, individual tribal councils, bands and native organizations can be found on any day engaged in a gritty battle with Child Welfare authorities to reclaim their children. Their hard-won successes at establishing child welfare programs are seldom celebrated in the media or on the conference floors where First Nations leaders gather. White politicians from Victoria and Ottawa are now seen traipsing from one Indian meeting to the next in an effort to be seen alongside First Nations leaders discussing the "land title" question. The media faithfully reports these events and focuses attention on First Nations leaders. Ironically, it is the ordinary First Nations families who are responsible for advancing the native title question to its current status. It was, after all, Ron Sparrow and his fellow band members who won the most significant ruling from the Supreme Court of Canada on the matter of native fishing rights. All the while, white politicians are scrambling to have their names associated with Indian leaders who had no direct hand in the success of decisions like "Sparrow."

In the offices of a major Indian organization in downtown Vancouver, a young Indian woman, Lizbeth Pointe, is hunched over her computer terminal looking for clues which will help reunite an Indian child adopted in the 1960s with his natural mother, who has been engaged in a three-decade long search for her lost child. Ms. Pointe's face lights up, she makes one telephone call and shouts, "Bingo!" She has just discovered the whereabouts of the child for which the mother had been searching for some twenty-seven years. She then telephones the mother, who is overwhelmed with emotion. Mother and child will eventually meet. Lizbeth Pointe returns her gaze to her desk and surveys the remaining 250 active files which contain the hopes of families looking for their lost children and the dreams of children looking for their families. Lizbeth Point sighs and returns to her computer terminal.

The Indian Act of 1876 was indeed the instrument which separated First Nations people from their tribal land holdings and Indian children from their parents. This legislation estranged Indians from whites and one

158

First Nation from another for over a century. Now the world has changed: not only are First Nations families reclaiming their children, they are also reclaiming their rightful place in Canada. Whites, who for a century systematically dispossessed Indians from the land, are now turning to the Indians for crucial lessons on how to live with the land. While tragic events involving Indian children continue to unfold, there is now hope the lives of aboriginal families will dramatically improve in the coming decades.

The day will soon come when First Nations people and whites will sit together to take part in the greatest potlatch of all. They will talk and sing about the wonderful world they will be leaving for their children. In the middle of the great feast hall two small figures will approach a fire. The feast hall will fall into silence. All eyes will be on the two children. One child will be white, the other will be brown. The children will raise a document over their heads. In the dim light of the feast hall, the title of the document will be seen and it will read, "The Indian Act." The two children will smile and gleefully toss the document which had kept their two peoples strangers to one another for more than a hundred years into the flames. A great cheer will sound in the feast hall.

Far off in Ottawa, a public servant in the Department of Indian Affairs will clean out his desk, walk to the door, turn off the lights, and turn the key in the lock for the last time.

BIBLIOGRAPHY

Albert, Jim. "Child Welfare. " In *The Canadian Encyclopedia*. Vol. I. A — For. Edmonton: Hurtig, 1985.

Castle, Henry. Private Conversation. September 11, 1990.

Comeau, Pauline, and Stantin, Aldo. *The First Canadian: A Profile of Canada's Native People Today*. Toronto: James Lorimer & Company, 1990.

Frideres, James S. *Canada's Indians: Contemporary Conflicts*. Scarborough: Prentice-Hall of Canada, 1974.

George, Margaret. Presentation at Cross-Cultural Workshop, Italian Cultural Centre, Vancouver, 5 October 1990.

Glavin, Terry. *A Death Feast in Dimlahamid*. Vancouver: New Star Books, 1990.

Haig-Brown, Celia. *Resistance and Renewal: Surviving the Indian Residential School*. Vancouver, Tillacum, 1988.

Johnson, Patrick. *Native Children and the Child Welfare System*. Toronto: Canadian Council on Social Development in association with James Lorimer & Company, 1983.

MacDonald, Neil. Interviews. 24 October 1988 and 24 May 1989.

Mathias, Chief Joe. "Conspiracy of Legislation." Mimeographed early version January 21, 1986.

Miller, J. R. *Skyscrapers Hide the Heavens. A History of Indian-White Relations in Canada*. Toronto: University of Toronto Press, 1989.

Tennant, Paul. *Aboriginal Peoples and Politics: The Indian Land Question in British Columbia, 1849-1989*. Vancouver: University of British Columbia, 1990.

More Than Us

As I was saying before I was so rudely interrupted,
The sea and land were created,
And, they continue to be created.
So were we . . . and so do we.

We depend upon the sea,
And give nothing back, except rarely.
We live upon the land,
And more or less give our bodies to it.

Women and men alone can not do it;
A greater power must bless them.
Then there is true love,
And the birth of a child will follow.

Our children are not just ours,
They come from more than just us,
And must return to something more or less
More than us.

Summer 1980,
at Aktiss,
for Queen

Native Spirituality, Past, Present, and Future

LEONARD GEORGE

"This, said the holy people, is where God talks to us; where we can dance with our spirit; where we can go into our past, present, and future; where we can be in touch with our loved ones far away."

QUTSAME is known to many as Leonard George. He is the youngest son of the late Chief Dan George. Leonard graduated from Notre Dame High School and then studied drama at Vancouver College for two years. He worked in theatre and movies until 1970, then as a labourer before becoming involved in native community work at the Vancouver Indian Centre. He established the Chief Dan George Memorial Foundation to train and develop native people in the film industry. For the past ten years Leonard has conducted workshops and seminars on native culture. He is currently the chief of the Burrard band and with his wife Susan is the proud parent of four sons.

* * *

Nature has many ways of creating balance and harmony. All living things have their place in the spectrum of life, and all living things have their own roles and functions. There is no confusion: genetic imprinting has made it very clear to all creatures who they are and what they must do in their life. The relationships among the creatures are also clearly defined, and it is a never-ending source of wonder to observers to see how well the creatures of the forest and other environments cohabit and contribute to the well-being of their worlds.

The only exception in nature is we human creatures, for we do not have a particular place and function in the life cycle. We have been given the great gift of conscious minds to determine and choose our directions in life. Because we aren't set in definite roles, we must construct our own relationships with the others in our environment. When we do not have a clear knowledge of what contributions can be made by each other, then we can encroach upon and duplicate each other's roles while leaving other necessary roles unfilled.

I believe that most of us share the vision of a balanced and harmonious life in a healthy world. To achieve this we must utilize all the strengths and capabilities of every human creature and we must develop our roles and relationships. This can only happen through the kind of deep understanding that results from serious dialogue and sharing. When we understand our differences and the things we have in common, then we may grow and survive together.

The aboriginal people of North America had a system in place that allowed them to live in this land for thousands of years. This system was based on spirituality. In this paper I will briefly describe the spirituality of aboriginal people, yesterday, today, and tomorrow.

To start I offer my personal definition of spirituality. Spirituality is the bringing together of those things that are essential to our becoming human beings. The human part of us is our body, and the being part is the spirit. Our purpose in life is to bring these together in the best possible way, as our Creator intended. The relationship between the body and the spirit is what makes us whole — all the other things we do are secondary to becoming the best possible human beings.

Past

Native North America was governed by spirituality prior to contact with the European in that all the leaders of the tribes and nations from east coast to west coast were holy people. These were people who regarded themselves as instruments of the Creator's work. To become an instrument, it was necessary to become humble like the water: always seeking the lowest places on earth, running around and beneath all things and yet remaining relentless in its efforts, always ongoing, never stopping yet when necessary having the power to move a mountain. When a person achieved this level of consciousness, that person was then a servant of mankind — a lover of mankind and thus a leader of people.

A leader has to assist people with their needs. But for this system to work, the individual people must live with the same values as the leader. For aboriginal people this meant the spiritual values which came from their relationship with the Great Spirit which said that your purpose in life was to become the best possible human being you could in your lifetime so that you could enter into an eternal life with the Creator.

The leaders taught that all the gifts we are born with are the tools that the Great Spirit has given us to succeed in life. We are born highly intelligent, loving, kind, generous, caring, sharing and honest. The leaders believed that if one embraced those qualities, he or she had everything needed to succeed in life. However, if one moved away and was selfish, uncaring, and dishonest, he or she would not achieve life's purpose.

162

The leaders also taught that to remain tuned and in the proper relationship, people must follow the Wheel of Life. This is the symbolic circle of the
universe which holds all together in relationship to one another, with
everything having a purpose and a balance to offset the other. It is fash-
ioned after the world itself, being balanced by the four directions, the four
races, and four human characteristics.

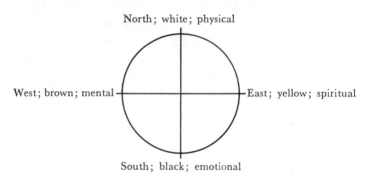

FIGURE 1

Wheel of Life

All the facets of the Wheel are related and in balance to each other,
beginning with our personal wheel, which includes the respect for all the
other parts of the Wheel.

So we start with our own physical, mental, spiritual, and emotional
being. Each of these aspects contributes to the wholesomeness of the next.
If you are happy and healthy in your physical self, you can love yourself.
People were taught to keep in shape, eat the right foods, and respect their
bodies, not hurting them in any way. The people knew that this gave the
best chance for the rest of your wheel to work. Because the native people
knew this, every one of their rituals, customs, and traditions complemented
each other and were enhanced by this holistic approach to life. Directions
for these practices came from the Creator and from the human leaders and
teachers, and the practices were all simple. The simplicity prevented a
myriad of complications within the body and spirit. It started with eating
pure, good food in adequate quantities to nourish, not stuff. The other
activities included running, fasting, meditation, singing, dancing, sweat-
lodge participation, pipe ceremonies, and cold water baths. Along with
keeping a healthy body, one tried to stay in balance with the environment
by rising when the sun came up, working and playing in the day, and rest-
ing when the sun went down: all simple processes which kept the people
well. This is strongly illustrated when one looks back at decades of native

lifestyles and sees the physical differences in the early pictures of the strong, noble native. It is also notable that at first contact, the life expectancy for European men was between 35 and 40 years, whereas among the native peoples there were often five generations living together, headed up by the aged great-grandparents. Unfortunately, this is not true today because, like most North Americans, aboriginal people have moved from good natural nutrition and exercise to poisoning their bodies with chemicals like sugar, alcohol, and drugs.

To return to the Wheel, you can see that if one is healthy physically, one also tends to be in good health mentally. Now all of the activities or, more appropriately, rituals mentioned in relation to the physical are also imperative to the well-being of the mental state. The mind is unlimited in potential to hold on to positive and negative information — wonderful philosophy or hazardous hurt. Each must be expressed in order to be wholesome.

We have been taught that the brain is divided in two interesting ways. The first is a division of right- and left-brain thinking. The right is our intuitive and dream half, which allows us a relationship with the mystical and the things we feel — those things we know but can't explain. The left is the logical and calculated planning side, where order is maintained and we plan our 1, 2, 3 approaches to keeping life regulated. Like all other things that are right in life, there is a balance in the brain functions. That is why it is important for all people to do activities that use both sides of the brain.

The holy people also taught that there are three levels of thinking and communicating. There is the conscious level, the one we are most familiar with. This is where we use our will deliberately to direct our thoughts and actions. There is the unconscious level, where we are aware of what we are doing but perhaps not aware that we chose to do it. This is when you find yourself involved in something but you are not sure why you are doing it. The third level is the subconscious — this is the level few people ever become familiar with because it requires intense meditation and listening over long periods of time before you start to consciously receive the messages from this level.

The holy people said that the answers to life are in the second and third levels of our mind, and they spent the majority of their lives trying to reach those levels because it is believed that this is where God talks to us. The rituals mentioned earlier — such as singing, dancing, swimming, sweats, meditation, pipe ceremonies, fasting, and long-distance running — are all activities that bring us to a physical state where it is much easier for us to reach our unconscious and subconscious minds. This, said the holy people, is where God talks to us; where we can dance with our spirit; where we can go into our past, present, and future; where we can be in touch with our loved ones far away.

These are the positives that result from using the power of the unconscious and subconscious person. The negative aspects are that we retain hurt, pain, worry, anger, revenge, and grief in these levels because all that comes at us is evaluated, registered, and stored as information until it is needed in our lives. If we store more negative than positive information, this causes major illness. All other conscious actions cease, the hurt prevents us from physically caring, we have no control of our emotions, and there is a lack of "will" to do or to talk to God. Also, this hurt stops new information from entering. Once again, this is where the tried and true rituals of the past assisted in maintaining health. They helped us to express our pain, sorrow, anger, or whatever. When we sing, we cannot help but sing with what we are feeling. It will come out on its own. It will be expressed and, once expressed, it will not burden us any longer and we will be relieved of that negative. We are not meant to hold all our feelings inside; we have a great need to express in order to stay whole. A good example is our babies; when they are hungry or hurt they cry, when they are happy they laugh, when the need comes they scream. In the man remains the boy and in the woman remains the girl, and no matter how old we get the child in us still needs to be nourished with love, understanding, caring, and encouragement.

A lot of the time we have to give ourself the opportunity to recognize which one of these needs requires our help. Here again, the rituals do this: they allow us to cry, scream, laugh or whatever. It is like a tune-up for a car: when we are cleaned physically and mentally we are able to control ourselves emotionally. The expression of emotion balances our feelings: if it was not good to laugh, it would not be good to cry. Anger balances happiness. We must, however, guide our feelings through the process until we are back to normal. Anger is a good emotion, but if not controlled it can be damaging to oneself and to whomever one may be dealing with. This damage is exactly what we need to avoid. So, it was taught, emotion is highly important and the traditional rituals central to allowing people to express emotion.

Understanding the importance of expressing emotion is particularly important for men today. There is so much emphasis on being macho that it prevents normal human acts like crying. Boys and men feel they have to be strong, that crying is not manly, which is so wrong (the old ones said, if it wasn't good to cry, it wouldn't be good to laugh). Men die early of heart attacks from holding on to what is meant to be expressed. Crying, laughing, anger, sorrow, loneliness, depression, fear and doubt are all emotions that need the opportunity to be expressed or released in various ways. When they are properly released, then the physical and mental emotions are healthy and we are much more likely to think of ourselves in a spiritual manner. Again, the rituals help because all of these activities and practices were answers to prayers to God on how to deal with the burdens and joys of being human. The holy people stressed that it was necessary to keep all things in balance because our purpose is to become the best possible human being in our lifetime so that we can enter into our eternal life with the Great Spirit.

At the height of the old system of life was a structure that was referred to as the Great Turtle. The native peoples of North America viewed their lands as Turtle Island, not because North America was shaped like a turtle but because it was considered the system upon which native people govern themselves, in that at the seven vital points of the turtle was a holy person who looked to the needs of the people and the land. The points were the head, right and left front legs, right and left hind legs, the tail and the heart. These positions from East to West and North to South of North America were held by holy people who provided spiritual guidance and leadership to their people, based upon a common set of values held by all the nations. The world and life of that time was by no means perfect, but there was a simple and effective system of helping humans in their struggles to be human beings which helped them and their environment survive for thousands of years.

Present

What happened, and why did this system stop? Largely it stopped because Europeans brought with them a system based on materialism. On "contact" with North America, this new system based on greed and power was introduced to the people living in North America. In order to give credibility to this system of material values, the native value system based on spiritual values had to be discredited and the people declared incompetent. In hindsight, we can easily say that the native people of North America were oppressed by three major forces. These were government, religion, and Hollywood.

Government first proclaimed that the natives were savage and followed pagan practices, which of course had to be stopped for the good of all. The first phase of the conquering and exploiting of the new land was to battle and exterminate the people to extinction if possible or, if not, at least to the point of control. So the new leaders began their quest to remove the Indian people from the way of progress. They killed off tribes of people and herds of animals, destroyed miles and miles of forests, contaminated water, burned vegetation, and made laws against speaking the native languages and practising the native traditions. Finally, the native rights to live with and move freely through the land were removed. Once these new conquerors had completed their task of killing and corralling natives, they established a number of institutions and procedures to ensure they maintained control over the lives of the aboriginal people. These included residential schools, reserves, and agencies like the Department of Indian Affairs, the failures of which have been very topical.

In retrospect it was not so much that native people were hated or not liked, it was just that they were in the way because they occupied the areas where virtually every major city in North America is now built. These were and are the most practical and best sites with water, trails, seas, rivers all at hand. To build the new cities and make them available for the new citizens, the businessmen and governments had to extinguish the rights and privileges of the aboriginal landholders. This was done first by war and then by assimilation. It should be remembered that Geronimo, Sitting Bull, Seattle, Walking Buffalo, Chief Sophie Pierre, Chief Dan George, Chief Joe Mathias and so on through history were not stoic chiefs, warmongers or savage; they were merely people fighting for their right to be human, to govern their people and maintain jurisdiction over their land.

The second oppressor is religion. This involves not so much Christians who are trying to live out their belief in God through religion but the dogma itself — the rules and regulations, the inability to recognize that there are many ways to talk to God and many rituals to bring people closer to God and to develop and enhance spirituality. The missionaries who ran the boarding schools had good intentions but were acting on false and unstudied information about natives. One of the biggest confusions for native people was the notion of the Fear of God — the concept of eternal punishment. In their own system, the Creator was the source where people had always gone for grace, guidance and strength.

The residential schools had a devastating impact. Families were separated, life skills lost, and family units dismantled, and loneliness and insecurity began to be harvested among children. Elders lost parenting skills, and children returned as strangers with different languages and values and no place to use the educations they had received. Because of the changed way of life, there was no longer a way for natives to make a living.

The reservations became North America's first ghettos, with poverty, disease, and abuse rampant. Both boarding schools and reserves pushed assimilation by fostering the idea that there was a much better life outside the traditional native community. The end result of all the efforts was a people who lost much of their language, their self-sufficiency, culture, traditions, land, family, and faith.

To add to this, along came the third oppressor — Hollywood. This means any kind of media or press, beginning with the early journalists and progressing through to film. The media established in people's minds an image of Indians so powerful and controlling that even today it is hard to rise above it. First, there is the romantic picture of feathers, beads, and noble warriors with supernatural powers and skills. Then there is the other image of ignorant, animal-like creatures that were dirty, cunning, unreliable, bloodthirsty beings that terrorized the plains, killing men, women and children, with no scruples whatsoever. As time passed, Indians came to be portrayed as drunken, lazy misfits. Always, they were portrayed as stereotypes, not as individuals. When you place human beings in a role category, you dehumanize them. That is what has been done by the media, and for a long time it was reinforced in educational books.

After years of oppression, it is no wonder that spiritual values have suffered and native people are low in spirit. But it is not only native people who have suffered a loss of spirit through oppression. It is all humans: white, black, yellow, and brown alike. The priority has become the processing of resources to make money, and human needs have become secondary. Native people have always believed that any nation's greatest asset is its people.

The future of spirituality is dependent on all of us, just as it was in the beginning. We all must take the individual responsibility to go back and restore our spiritual values. Before this can happen in North America, we must have a healing between native and non-native peoples. First, however, each of the races will have to heal itself. Here in North America we have a better opportunity than anywhere else in the world because we have the freedom to work for change.

The first step is to tell you that before contact with the Europeans had ever taken place, it was prophesied that a great healing would take place, starting with the heart of the turtle, which is the Hopi people in Arizona. The prophecy said, "A huge wave of white people will come and with their coming the native spirit will be wiped out to almost nothing, but when it hits its lowest point the Indian spirit would start to rise up again and out of this new rising would come not only strong brown Indians but white

Indians. The beginning of this new rising would be signified by the eagle landing on the moon." In 1969, when the first spacecraft landed on the moon, the first words spoken were "the Eagle has landed." This coincided with a number of other social and political events that started the unchaining of native spirit. This momentous achievement also seemed to stimulate a lot of reflection on lifestyles and direction among the non-natives. This kind of reflection starts people on their Wheel of Life. The past twenty years have seen enormous changes in the way people eat, care for themselves, and seek spiritual enlightenment.

The very first realization we must make is that the spiritual can balance the material and that neither has to be a burden. Second, we as people have to acknowledge that some very real things have happened in history to weaken us. But having acknowledged that, we must not continue to use our hurt as an excuse for inaction. We must use our past experiences as good reasons to succeed. We must learn to become hunters of the city, in the way our ancestors were hunters of the forest: by approaching everyone and everything with respect, never taking more than we need, always giving back something, and always being thankful. Successful hunters of the past brought home their take, took what they required, and shared the rest with the less fortunate. If we apply this in the city, it changes our attitude, because if we only seek what we need, selfishness and greed are removed, and the frustration of expecting more is eliminated.

Material values don't have to control us. We can find the strength to stand up for our human rights and needs. By loving, caring, and sharing, with honesty and by listening to our heart and mind, we can know what is right. We must stop living in criticism of one another as humans and stop alienating one another. Although we are different races, we share many things spiritually and materialistically. In our spirit we fear and are brave, we laugh and we cry, we mourn and rejoice. On the material plane, we worry about hydro bills, car payments, and our children's needs. There are so many ways we are bound by common concerns. These should keep us together, working for the common good of our earth, water, and air and, most importantly, our future generations of humans.

First we must love ourselves, then we can love each other; respect ourselves so we can respect each other. Within every woman remains the girl, and within every man remains the boy who must be nourished, encouraged, and understood. Each of us must take responsibility for making changes and using his or her spiritual values. Once more, as in the beginning, we must be wise enough to follow the teachings of the Holy People and be healed. Then the balance so needed for life will be restored.

Telling

We long for a new reading of history.
We wax nostalgic.
We wish the newsreels of history
Could be rewound, run backwards
Before our eyes.

Warriors would drop their rifles.
Constructed residential schools
Could be deconstructed.
Dying languages would find
Our throats once more.
The Indian Act would be unwritten.

Perhaps our worth would be known,
Our intellect revealed and
Recognized as needed.
We long for a new telling of history.

Such a story would remain our own,
A fire ashore at night.
Gentle and honest and telling,
Before all eyes.

Fall 1988,
at Musqueam